THE NATIONAL TRUST GUIDE

LAWNS &
GROUND COVER

THE NATIONAL TRUST GUIDE

LAWNS &
GROUND COVER

STEPHEN LACEY
────── SERIES EDITOR ──────
PENELOPE HOBHOUSE

PAVILION

Published in association with
THE NATIONAL TRUST
36 Queen Anne's Gate
London SW1H 9AS

First published in Great Britain in 1991 by
PAVILION BOOKS LIMITED
196 Shaftesbury Avenue, London WC2H 8JL

Text copyright © Stephen Lacey 1991
Photographic credits listed on page 110

Designed by Elizabeth Ayer

A CIP catalogue record for this book is
available from the British Library.

ISBN 1 85145 295 8

Printed and bound in Italy
New Interlitho, Milan

10 9 8 7 6 5 4 3 2 1

PAGE 2: *The rhododendron woodland at* BODNANT GARDEN, *Gwynedd.*

CONTENTS

INTRODUCTION

Gardening is no fun if you feel a yoke on your back. It is essential that you are able to enjoy pottering in the greenhouse or herbaceous border, vegetable garden or rock garden, or for that matter swinging idly in your hammock, without feeling that you ought to be getting on with chores. To free yourself for the activities you enjoy most, you have to designate certain other parts of the garden as low-maintenance areas.

Paving, grass, ground cover and 'natural' planting are the most labour-saving treatments. These are the subjects of this book and the gardens of the National Trust are its inspiration. Water, another option, is a subject worthy of a book of its own.

The National Trust gardens are a rich source of ideas, both aesthetic and practical. They may be larger and grander in concept than our own, but many of their design and planting details are easily reduced in scale and adapted for the garden at home. Sometimes a section of garden provides a fine blueprint for the layout of your entire garden – the 'rooms' of compartmented gardens like SNOWSHILL, HIDCOTE and SISSING-HURST are no bigger than many suburban plots.

The National Trust gardening staff is the country's greatest pool of practical horticultural wisdom. Because of the size and complexity of the gardens they maintain, the gardeners are usually as short of time as we are (NT properties never have as many gardeners as you think). Consequently, they put into practice many labour-saving treatments which ordinary gardeners can pick up.

Although paving, grass, ground cover and natural planting can be the passport to leisure, they can also be the source of lasting pleasure. The ground pattern of paving, grass, plants and water underpins every garden. It furnishes the horizontal plane, sets the scene and provides a backdrop.

The paved areas can help to link the house to its surroundings by echoing its stone or brickwork in the garden. Paths set courses for the eye as well as the feet; by following straight lines they can help impose formal order on the site, by curving out of sight they can be a gentle encouragement to explore. Choosing appropriate materials and planning how and where you are going to lay them is a real design challenge. Beautiful features can encourage the family to make more use of the garden by providing places for sitting out and outdoor entertaining.

Grass areas also need to be carefully shaped. Closely mown lawns, in geometrical or abstract form, can be the garden's central arena, a quiet green oasis between flower-packed borders or an antidote to built-up surroundings. Used in broad sweeps and narrow paths, grass can also be a dynamic force, leading the eye to a view or to another feature, and providing the neutral carpet which unites the garden's various parts. And, of course, it offers a soft, hard-wearing surface which can be used for various activities.

Ground-cover planting can be as colourful and as full of seasonal incident as other types of planting. The difference is

The formal Theatre Lawn at
HIDCOTE MANOR, Gloucestershire provides a
tranquil respite from the colourful flower borders. Grass,
hedges and trees can make a complete composition, which is
satisfying to look at in all seasons.

only that you are using plants which largely look after themselves and keep weeds at bay. Accordingly, it too requires sensitive planning – in the way beds are shaped, heights are distributed, and colours and textures are juxtaposed.

And natural planting can produce absorbing woodland, pondside and meadow communities of flowers and foliage. With careful planning, you can merge your garden imperceptibly with the countryside around it, or create a valuable urban haven for wildlife.

So these topics deserve to be considered with a designer's, plantsman's and practical gardener's eye and I have tried to give them rounded treatment in this book. It has been extremely instructive for me, preoccupied as I am with the intricacies of ornamental planting, to focus on matters outside my usual sphere as I have visited National Trust gardens. And perhaps I may be able to encourage you on your future visits occasionally to direct your eyes away from the immediately eye-catching attractions, and to consider the way the paving, grass and areas of simple and relaxed planting are quietly contributing to the garden's mood and character.

LEFT: *At BARRINGTON COURT,
Somerset, the mellow orange-brown brick of the
house is also used for garden walls and paths. House and
garden are thus fused together imperceptibly. Marigolds
and heleniums add to the harmony by echoing
the tints of the brick.*

RIGHT: Alchemilla mollis *and hostas used as ground cover at
ACORN BANK GARDEN, Cumbria.*

PAVED AREAS AND PATHS

There is no doubt that paving is the most labour-saving ground-cover treatment. Its other attributes are that it gives hard, all-weather standing and provides an alternative to lawn in areas which are too shady for grass, too fiddly to mow and suffer too much human traffic. It can also be an attractive feature in its own right.

If you have a very small garden, you should think hard whether you want grass at all. Lawns are usually hopeless in inner city gardens, for instance. The sites are invariably dry and shady and are heavily used for sitting out and entertaining. What is more, their owners have little inclination to mow after a hard day at the office and are frequently away at weekends. Paving is the obvious treatment.

Mrs Winthrop's Garden at HIDCOTE MANOR illustrates how a small garden may be attractively designed without using grass. The whole enclosure is paved in brick, except for four flowerbeds which are filled with plants with blue or yellow flowers. The site is square but the groundplan revolves around a circular brick arena, set slightly below ground level. An ornamental pot containing a dramatic architectural specimen (usually a bronze cordyline) provides the pivot for the design. An expanse of brick paving can appear cold and severe, but here any such tendency is countered by the abundance of plant material, especially lime-green *Alchemilla*

Mrs Winthrop's Garden, one of HIDCOTE'S *many compartments, is a fine blueprint for a small garden. With its central circle and focal point – a bronze cordyline (cabbage palm) – its clear colour scheme, and surrounding hedges, the design is simple and self-contained.*

mollis, which spills out of the beds, softens the edges and provides an unruly antidote to the disciplined groundplan.

In larger gardens, your open spaces will be laid mainly to grass – for aesthetic and financial reasons – but paved areas remain essential for day-to-day living and you will want to incorporate them into the design somewhere. The obvious and most convenient location will be close to the house, where the garden will anyway tend to be more formal and obviously man-made. The grander National Trust properties have impressive expanses of hard standing around them, set about with seats, decorated with statuary, and sometimes even embroidered with a parterre or knot garden. At ASHDOWN HOUSE, for example, clean rectangles of gravel anchor the Restoration house in its grounds and offer all-weather access to all sides. The gravel is free of incident on three sides of the house – apart from tubs of clipped box – but on the fourth side a simple box parterre has been recently laid out.

Other Trust properties have more homely sitting-out areas, and these furnish us with more practical ideas. PACKWOOD has a tiny paved area, snugly enclosed by the high walls of the house and garden. It is a shallow rectangle, partitioned from the lawn by low brick walls and steps, and laid with stone slabs. Much of the charm is due to its intimate size and to the presence of climbing roses on the walls, which soften the architecture and, most importantly, contribute scent. Of all the places in the garden to grow scented plants, the sitting-out area comes top. It is here that night-scented flowers should be grouped to catch your attention as you take your evening drink, and fragrant-leaved plants sited so you can tweak them as you sit.

Gravel reflects the sunlight and complements the brick walls in the north forecourt at WEST GREEN HOUSE, *Hampshire. Statues and fastigiate yews prevent monotony and lend a touch of theatre.*

The classic width for a paved area adjacent to the house is half the house's height. Often it is preferable to equal the height for a really luxurious effect. The more generous the space, the more conducive to relaxation it will be and, after all, this is the place for unwinding and for idle pleasure. This is also the reason for opting for a static, balanced design. Self-contained geometrical patterns are invariably more satisfactory here than restless abstract ones.

The materials with which such areas are constructed must also be harmonious and easy on the eye. Brick paviors, engineering and paving bricks, stone and exposed aggregate concrete slabs, granite setts, cobbles and gravel are all candidates. They come in many shapes and colours, and can be laid, either in isolation or mixed with other materials, in many different patterns. Inspiration should be drawn from the building materials of your house, its architectural detail and the spirit of the garden around.

Paved areas need not be just bare expanses of hard surfacing. Plants from neighbouring borders should over-flow on to them and plants on the house walls should contribute a backdrop of flowers and foliage. But you can also set features into the paving. You can introduce a centrepiece – a lily pond, for example (water, either calm or gently moving, soothes the mind and encourages contemplation) – or an arrangement of flowerbeds; if you have no room for beds, leave cracks in the paving for bushy aromatic thymes, lavender and chamomile and for vertical accent plants like dieramas, sea hollies (*Eryngium*) and irises.

Terracotta pots, stone troughs and wooden tubs planted with annuals and tender perennials are an excellent way of bringing summer gaiety on to the paving. The garden at POWIS CASTLE is a rich source of inspiration for container planting, really opening your eyes to the extent of plant material available and the many stunningly beautiful ways of using it.

Statuary and furniture also brings interest. Lead figures and cisterns, stone urns and balustrades and even old laundry coppers feature in Trust gardens. Many different

For an informal effect leave cracks in the paving for aromatic plants and self-seeders.

Terracotta pots are an excellent way of bringing summer gaiety to a paved area.

Well Court at SNOWSHILL MANOR, Gloucestershire, is a small, formally designed enclosure comprising stone, grass, water, relaxed cottage planting, and a well head as the centrepiece.

styles of seat and table are available, and they can be painted in any colour, one of the most pleasing shades being Wade Blue, a turquoise-tinted blue used on the wooden furniture at SNOWSHILL and named after the garden's creator Charles Wade.

Topiary is a cheaper means of introducing ornament and architectural substance. You do not expect to see topiary figures on paving but there is no reason why they cannot feature in place of traditional knots and parterres. On the gravel terrace at NYMANS, in front of the ruins of the Great Hall, are some box birds which look as if they have alighted directly out of the pages of *Alice in Wonderland*.

The provision of shade may also be important, though the British are by nature sun-worshippers and only on rare really scorching days are we likely to seek refuge; a few seats under a tree will probably be sufficient. But vine-clad pergolas are a welcome addition in hotter climates.

Grass can also be introduced into paved areas to soften the groundplan. It can take the form of an enclosed lawn – perhaps a circular centrepiece or a pair of symmetrical rectangles – or it can be fully integrated to make an intricate pattern. At KNIGHTSHAYES a geometrical pattern of grass and paving is so well balanced that it is hard to decide whether this is a lawn intersected by paths or a paved area decorated with grass. At GREYS COURT there is a turf and brick maze, representing the path of life.

TERRACES

If your land slopes, you will have to terrace it in order to obtain a flat area for paving. If this is feasible, physically and financially, it is always worth doing. Again, the width of the terrace will ideally be equivalent to at least half the height of the house, but if the slope is steep, it is better to plan a series of shallower terraces rather than have one enormous terrace requiring a monstrous retaining wall for support.

The greatest terrace gardens were created in Italy during the Renaissance. Carved out of the steep hillside, they link the architecture of the house with the surrounding landscape

A spring view of part of the small terrace at KNIGHTSHAYES COURT *in Devon, with its geometrical pattern of grass and paving.*

Magnificent Italianate terracing at POWIS CASTLE, *lavishly planted, forges a link between the imposing sandstone castle and its pastoral platform.*

and provide a series of stages for enjoying the drama of the terrain and for contemplating and marvelling at man's inventiveness and artistry in sculpture and design.

In Britain, perhaps the most elegant Italianate terraces are at POWIS CASTLE. Its gardens were designed in the late seventeenth century, so that terraces led from the imposing red sandstone castle to the great empty lawn at the bottom, offering magnificent views across the Shropshire hills. They incorporate an orangery and an aviary, lead figures, and a

dazzling display of lush herbaceous plants and uncommon shrubs.

The terraces at BODNANT were made this century, and are much broader. Each has its own special character and is retained by walls of chunky granite, festooned with climbing plants. The scale of the garden is breathtaking, and the views across to the mountains of Snowdonia suitably majestic. But even here there are touches for the ordinary gardener to pick up – such as the use of pendent wisteria (and a small waterfall) to echo the cascading effect of the terraces and remind you that you are in the process of a substantial descent.

Also grand and impressive, but in quite a different way, is the 'terrace' at CRAGSIDE. The house is perched precariously on a steep hill and the terrace is little more than a ledge on the side of a cliff, overlooking the wooded valley. A small section has been covered in paving setts but otherwise the terrace is constructed with immense flat-topped boulders. What a romantic place to take breakfast!

More homely terracing is evident at COTEHELE, where sloping paths flank a formal garden on four levels. On the flat ground are lawns and rose beds, and aubrieta grows in the short retaining walls. Below the terraces is a steep-sided valley, where the slopes are thick with trees, rhododendrons and other flowering shrubs, and, as in the woodland valley garden at BODNANT, offer complete contrast to the formality beside the house.

An attraction of retaining walls for the plantsman is that they make wonderful homes for alpine plants, which relish the sharp drainage. Capitalizing on this, the small terraces below the Paved Garden at KNIGHTSHAYES have been turned into alpine beds. It seems to me that this is really the only way to grow such plants – formally, in a terraced design – in regions which are not naturally mountainous and where a rockery can only look artificial. Similarly, at ACORN BANK a wonderful miniature composition of a terraced lawn and dry stone walls is exploited to the full as a habitat for alpines. These prosper especially well in the vertical walls – in the wet climate of the north-west they are apt to rot when grown on the flat.

In shadier, less formal parts of the garden, peat blocks can be used as low retaining walls. They are particularly in evidence in the Woodland Garden at KNIGHTSHAYES, where they have been colonized by countless perennials including numerous ferns.

The main terraces at KNIGHTSHAYES are in front of the house. The top two are connected not by a retaining wall but by a grass slope. Slopes can look attractive as part of a terrace sequence and, of course, are a cheaper option, but they can be awkward to manage if they are grassed; the most labour-saving treatment is to use ground-cover planting.

At the bottom of this series of terraces is a ha-ha. This ingenious eighteenth-century conceit employs a retaining wall to lift the end of the garden above the countryside beyond, or a ditch to separate lawn from field. No barrier is visible from the garden side and the impression received is that the property extends much farther than it really does.

There is an example of a small-scale ha-ha at SNOWSHILL which gives a glimpse, between a hedge of holly and elder and mounds of ivy and cotoneaster, of the Gloucestershire countryside outside the garden. Here is proof that a design idea borrowed from the grandest gardens can easily be adapted and reduced in scale for home use, and with delightful consequences.

Sloping land makes a garden interesting and there is no need to despair if terracing is impractical and a flat paved area impossible. Even a garden treated conventionally with straight paths and formal beds is pleasing on a slope. The walled Mulberry Garden at BATEMAN'S, with its rectangular lawns and flowerbeds, slopes to the south, as does the formal box-edged Rose Garden at POLESDEN LACEY. The walled garden at WALLINGTON is a wonderful example of the drama sloping ground can bring to a groundplan; the upper part of the garden is terraced but below the gradient is steep and the lawns veer sharply to the south and the east.

From a plantsman's point of view, it is worth mentioning the special attraction of sloping ground facing south, south-east, west or south-west. Because of the acute angle to the sun, flowerbeds enjoy greater radiation. This keeps the soil warmer and promotes earlier growth in the spring. Also, a good slope ensures that frost, which flows like water and settles in the lowest pockets, runs off freely. These characteristics are exploited fully in the vegetable beds at several National Trust gardens, including TRENGWAINTON and UPTON HOUSE.

The Mexican daisy, ERIGERON KARVINSKIANUS, *is an adept colonizer and is seen here seeding into the steps at* HINTON AMPNER, *Hampshire. It blooms all summer.*

But whether you are terracing or whether you are retaining a slope with a sharp gradient, you will, unless you are a mountaineer, need to construct steps. Steps can be built using a variety of materials and should harmonize with their surroundings. They can be curved or straight, broad or narrow, shallow or steep. Just as in planning the course of a path, the determining factors are the lie of the land, the formality of the groundplan, and the pace at which you want to travel; steps that are broad in width and shallow in height are luxurious and invite slow progress, while narrow, steep steps demand energy and encourage speed.

A flight of steps used in conjunction with a retaining wall can flow at right angles to the wall and carry you forwards down the slope – as at the top of the Red Borders at HIDCOTE,

where the stone steps participate in a main axial line, which concludes in a ha-ha. Or it can hug the wall for all or part of its descent. The steps from the Orangery Terrace at POWIS CASTLE are in straight flights which cling to the walls and keep you sideways to the slope. But at NYMANS you are taken up to the Walled Garden by a stone flight of steps which curves like a staircase in a grand mansion; it is a double staircase, allowing you to climb either from the left or the right.

Steps themselves can also be curved, even as part of an otherwise linear flow. At PACKWOOD there is a most attractive example of a flight of semicircular steps at the end of a straight brick path. Indeed, the combination of circles with squares and rectangles is invariably pleasing in a garden's groundplan.

Flights of steps can also feature in a sloping path, to help you navigate a particularly steep section. You will encounter them in all the Trust's woodland gardens; the steps are usually hardcore and gravel, supported by railway sleepers, split logs or treated wood. At COTEHELE, chestnut palings, split and stored for 18 months (but not treated), are nailed on to the front of railway sleepers, to harmonize better with the sylvan setting.

Wooden ramps may also need to be considered for the convenience of disabled friends and members of the family. They can be an alternative to steps or used in conjunction with them. A highly successful idea at BATEMAN'S is to use a slatted wooden ramp over a grass bank. You can mow over the ramp and it blends perfectly with its surroundings, but it offers grip and a firm surface for wheelchairs.

PATHS

Entrance drives and the garden's main service paths also require covering with a hard, all-weather material. For drives tarmac will probably be the most attractive option, but remember that this need not be black. At DUNSTER terracotta-red tarmac has been used so that there is harmony with the sandstone walls of the castle; this is a colour that would tone

A circular flight of brick steps leads you to the yew garden at PACKWOOD HOUSE, *Warwickshire.*
Many garden designs are a clear play on geometrical shapes: here the curves of the steps contrast with the
straight-edged walls and pillars but are echoed in the urns and in the yews beyond.

well with many shades of house brickwork. Gravel-rolled tarmacs are also available now.

For footpaths, the same materials are available as those used for terraces and paved areas. York stone slabs are particularly in evidence in Trust properties, but these are usually prohibitively expensive and most of us would have to use reconstituted stone or textured concrete instead. Nevertheless, they remain the aristocrats of paving material and if you see any going cheaply, snap them up; their drawback is that they are slippery in wet weather and you may have to cover them with a thin layer of grit or sand in the winter.

But there are fine alternatives, which you can employ by themselves or mix together in imaginative mosaics. A horoscope has been inserted into a stone path at SNOWSHILL, for example, and you can see millwheels in brick paths in many Trust gardens including BATEMAN'S and BARRINGTON COURT. There is an unusual path of mixed stones and cobbles in the Cherry Garden at GREYS COURT, which is edged in brick and has old saddle stones set into it. An intricate cobblestone pattern can be seen on the floor of the grotto at STOURHEAD. And at ANTONY HOUSE stones are laid through a cobble path like stepping stones in a stream; this is a Japanese idea and runs beside the little Japanese garden there. Being uncomfortable to walk on, cobbles are often used in gardens to discourage visitors from taking particular routes.

Gravel surfacing is a relatively economical option and accounts for about three-quarters of all hard surfaces in National Trust gardens. Usually the gravel comes from regional quarries and the different types vary greatly in texture and colour. In its loose form, gravel can be irritating. It is easily scattered, especially by machines, where it abuts lawns; on steep ground it is easily washed away by rain; it is carried into the house by shoes; and it presents difficulties to wheelchair users. But the great joy of gravel from a plantsman's point of view is that plants love seeding themselves into it, and it gives you the opportunity of blending path and flowerbed perfectly. At KNIGHTSHAYES, the terraced alpine beds are cleverly integrated through the use of gravel as a mulch and as the medium for the path below; plants grow in both.

For paths and hard standing, compacted hoggins, consisting of different-sized pebbles mixed with clay, and binding gravels are the best choice. Among the former, Wormsheath hoggin, used at CLAREMONT, produces a very satisfactory surface glistening with rounded pebbles of all sizes.

Cornish elvan gravel is used at LANHYDROCK and is less slippery and dazzling than pea gravel. It is pink when quarried but turns bluish in the rain. Limestone chippings will bind to make a very good surface and are often available locally; the Lincoln terrace path at CLUMBER is an example. Pale Breedon gravel from Northamptonshire, available throughout Britain, is common in Trust gardens, and may be seen in the Flower Garden at CALKE ABBEY. And gravel scalpings, the waste from gravel chippings, are frequently used on the paths in woodland gardens. It is compacted by a roller to bind with the soil below.

My own favourite hard material for paths is brick. It is sympathetic, versatile and, because the units are small, easy to adapt to the eccentricities of your site. Old bricks are desirable because of their mellow appearance but there is a fine range of modern paviors available which are perfectly satisfactory and generally much tougher. Brick can be laid in all sorts of interesting patterns – from stretcher bond to herringbone – and the garden to visit in order to see the possibilities is BARRINGTON COURT, where the paths have each been individually and lovingly designed.

Paving always introduces order and a touch of formality into its setting, even if this is quite wild; gravel paths have this effect in the rough areas of BUSCOT. Where you want to preserve an informal and natural air, therefore, hard surfacing will be inappropriate. Away from the house, between trees and shrub borders, softer treatment is called for.

This sloping gravel path at SNOWSHILL MANOR
is softened by the billowing growth of herbaceous plants,
including campanulas, hollyhocks and alchemilla.

The Fuchsia Garden at HIDCOTE MANOR *is designed as a parterre, with a
symmetrical pattern of brick paths and box-edged flowerbeds. Hardy fuchsias, interplanted with scillas for
spring colour, provide a permanent, and labour-saving, bedding scheme.*

Grass paths are successful where there is ample light. Mowing is an unavoidable chore but edging need not be, if you take a more casual attitude and allow the grass to grow long at the sides and filter under the neighbouring shrubs; you can use a strimmer here now and again instead. In darker settings, a straightforward earth and hardcore path, perhaps topped with chipped bark, is attractive. This is really the one of the best options on sloping ground in woodland gardens, and such paths abound in Trust properties. Alternatively, binding gravel is perfectly good provided that there are occasional box drains.

Should your paths be straight or winding? Both practical and aesthetic factors will influence your decision. A general principle of design is that the garden becomes gradually less formal as you move away from the house; straight paths, together with borders of the more exotic flowers, give way to gentle curves and more natural plantings of shrubs and trees. But in small gardens this principle is not easy to follow, and your groundplan may employ both straight and winding paths in succession. As long as your overall design is coherent and there is a reason for each line and curve, the mix will be successful.

Straight paths take you quickly and directly from one point to another. Main service paths should be as straight as possible, especially the one leading from the garage to the back door and the one to the compost heap. There is nothing more irritating than being led on a merry ramble when you are struggling with bags of heavy shopping or a sack of lawn clippings. If the paths are not straight, corners will anyway tend to be cut by hurrying feet. Kitchen gardens also benefit from straight access paths, which facilitate manoeuvres with the wheelbarrow.

Otherwise the choice of a straight path is purely aesthetic. Straight paths bring discipline to the groundplan and are a wonderful influence on borders packed with wispy flowers or unruly herbs. They set a clear route for the eye and by being tapered or broadened at the end, they will respectively exaggerate or foreshorten distance.

It is very important, though, that paths which carry you off purposefully should lead somewhere interesting. A straight path should always end climactically in a view, a gateway, a seat or some other architectural or vegetable focal point. All the straight paths in the compartmented gardens of SISSING-HURST and HIDCOTE, for example, conclude in statues or seats, doorways or views. In grander Trust gardens they end in temples or pavilions, lakes or follies. Even the paths in vegetable gardens should terminate properly; in the kitchen garden at GREYS COURT one path carries you to an unusual octagonal Swiss fountain, guarded by eight 'Skyrocket' junipers.

If you need a straight path but are worried that it may make the garden look too formal, remember that you can soften it with planting. The central paths of the vegetable garden at TINTINHULL, one concluding in a gated entrance to a

A corner of Well Court at SNOWSHILL, *bright with Japanese anemones in late summer.*

cider orchard and the other in a stone urn, are lined respectively with catmint and the pink polyantha rose 'Nathalie Nypels' and the result is a delightfully romantic composition. For a more casual effect, use a mixed collection of plants to spill over the paving.

Another option is to construct an overhead canopy of foliage which conceals the severity of the design and, by playing with sunlight and shadow, creates mystery and drama. At BATEMAN'S a spacious ironwork tunnel, clad in pear trees, clematis and honeysuckles, arches over a brick path; at NYMANS an angular pergola of wisteria filters sunlight on to the paving stones below; at BODNANT laburnums are trained on metal hoops over a stone walkway; and at MOSELEY OLD HALL a beautiful wooden arbour spans a gravel path – it is draped in claret vine (*Vitis vinifera* 'Purpurea') which, when seen on a sunny day and from inside the arbour, becomes a spectacular scarlet.

Alternatively you can have a natural canopy formed by trees, such as in the Cherry Garden at GREYS COURT, where weeping white cherries make an intricate tracery of branches over the stones and cobbles. There is a tunnel of clipped hornbeam at LYTES CARY and, at WALLINGTON, one of yew. Interestingly, the latter has a valuable functional as well as aesthetic purpose: it spans a sloping path and prevents this icing over in winter and so becoming hazardous.

Of course, sometimes you will want to emphasize the lines of a straight path, and so give the groundplan the firm stamp of order. A tunnel or pergola can achieve this if it has strong uprights regularly spaced. The repetition of a feature carries the eye swiftly forwards. An avenue of trees is similarly effective, and so is a procession of uniform shrubs; the avenue of pudding-shaped box bushes at TINTINHULL is a famous formalizing feature. A hedge or pair of hedges flanking the path also reinforces the route by providing an additional line or lines.

A broken path of cobbles and stones at GREYS COURT, *Oxfordshire, emphasizes the mysterious pattern of sunlight and shadow created by the arching cherry trees.*

A path curves enticingly out of sight in the Walled Garden at WALLINGTON. *The corner is justified by shrubs but the grass and low planting on the other side retains space.*

Winding paths make progress more leisurely and give a more casual air to the groundplan. Topography will often dictate curves rather than straight lines, and the natural features and undulations of the site – which should always be seen as a source of inspiration rather than of problems – set an exact course for you. If there is no governing topography and winding paths are to be used, each curve needs to be justified with plants or architectural objects; there is nothing odder than a path which changes direction for no reason.

For entrance drives and broad walks, the curves are best made generous and gentle; intricate and meandering courses are for areas where you want to keep the pace deliberately slow – usually where rich flora needs to be savoured slowly. You can clearly see this principle followed at TRENGWAINTON, where the entrance drive and the footpath through the Woodland Garden run downhill parallel with the stream. Both have their course set by the stream, but whereas the drive whisks you majestically from house to gate by means of bold curves, the footpath twists at every rhododendron and camellia and encourages you to stop and enjoy each plant in turn.

Paths are always dynamic, but those that move in sweeping curves are particularly exciting to the eye. Look down towards the gatehouse from the Woodland Garden at LANHYDROCK and you will see an entrance drive surge with the force of a river, as it curves through the park and turns through the gate. More intricate winding paths excite in a different way, by leading you into the unknown, by playing hide and seek with plants, features and views, and by offering tantalizing glimpses of pleasures beyond. Again, those at LANHYDROCK are fine examples; as you walk along paths in the hillside garden, rich with the colour and scent of azaleas and rhododendrons, you look down and up at more paths, running parallel, descending, climbing and turning and enticing you on to further exploration.

Unlike straight paths, winding paths do not have to come to a climactic conclusion. Indeed, they can simply twist and

PAVING WHEEL

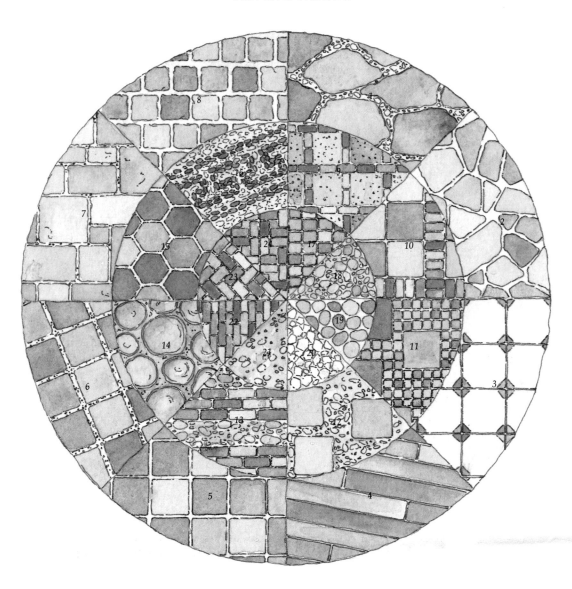

1. Natural Grey Stone
2. Crazy Paving
3. Ceramic Tiles
4. Timber Decking
5. Concrete Slabs (smooth)
6. Concrete Slabs (exposed aggregate)

7. York Stone
8. Granite Setts
9. Concrete/Brick
10. Brick/Slabs
11. Slabs/Granite Setts
12. Slabs/Gravel

13. Brick/Cobbles
14. Timber Rounds
15. Quarry Tiles
16. Stone Mosaic
17. Blue Brick
18. Pea Shingle

19. Cobbles
20. Limestone Chippings
21. Hoggin
22. Stretcher Bow Brick
23. Herringbone
24. Bedding Faces Brick

turn and bring you back to where you started. But they should not be an anticlimax, leading you to a dead end or, after a long walk, forcing you to retrace your footsteps. Ideally, you will always be carried forwards full of anticipation, and every so often be teased with a choice of direction.

PRACTICAL MATTERS

Having decided on the shape and extent of paved areas for your garden, on the arrangement of paths, the height of retaining walls and the location of steps, and having decided what materials to use, you are then faced with the job of construction. Paths and paved areas need a firm foundation. In the average garden, where they are not subject to heavy wear, a layer of builder's sand laid on top of the rolled and levelled ground may be a sufficient base for stone and brick paving.

But for the best results a layer of compacted hardcore 75mm / 3in thick, beneath a 25mm / 1in layer of sand, is preferable for stone and concrete slab paving. Brick and other small unit paving benefit from the same depth of foundation but the layer of sand may be substituted for dry mortar mix. Finally, sand – or, for brick paving, dry mortar mix – is brushed into the cracks.

For entrance drives, standing areas for vehicles, and other areas subject to heavy use, a more solid underlay will be required. A 100mm / 4in layer of consolidated hardcore and a 75mm / 3in bed of dry mortar mix gives the extra strength.

Binding gravel surfacing also benefits from a compacted hardcore foundation of at least 75mm / 3in. The hoggin or gravel is then spread in layers on top of this, each layer rolled and watered, to a compacted depth equal to the hardcore foundation. A selected finish of loose gravel or chippings, 12mm / ½in deep, may then be added.

Gravel and hoggin surfacing needs to be contained within rigid edging, made of pre-cast concrete or wooden boards and pegs. This is a sound policy when laying small unit paving too, and bricks stood on end serve as a good edging for brick paths.

Drainage is an important consideration. Paved areas must always slope slightly, and a cross gradient of about 1 in 60 for stone and brick, and 1 in 40 for gravel and hoggin, are recommended. Paths can slope from the side or from the centre, as the mounded tarmac paths do at STANDEN; where drains catch the rainwater and carry it down the slope in pipes. In the steep hardcore paths at STOURHEAD, slit drains

FOUR DIFFERENT PAVING SURFACES

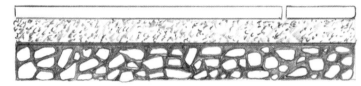

Large slabs of paving stone above mortar and then hardcore make a suitably hardwearing surface for a driveway.

Shallow foundations may be used for paths and patio areas.

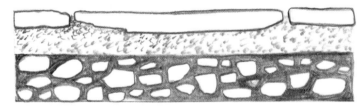

Natural stone paving over layers of sand and hardcore creates a less formal look, and small plants can be introduced into the crevices.

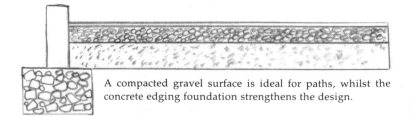

A compacted gravel surface is ideal for paths, whilst the concrete edging foundation strengthens the design.

have been inserted to take rainwater into the woodland beds and prevent the paths turning into rivers during heavy rain.

When constructing a flight of steps, you must first calculate the number of steps required by measuring the drop and dividing it by the height of the appropriate risers. The most comfortable flights of steps have risers around 150mm / 6in high and treads around 375mm / 15in deep.

BUILDING STEPS ON LEVEL GROUND

The first riser is laid on a concrete foundation.

The treads are fixed with mortar

Using hardcore as backfilling.

Risers less than 112mm / 4½in high are awkward to navigate; and 300mm / 12in is the minimum depth for treads. The shallower the treads, the higher the risers need to be.

If you are working on a slope, you can either cut out the whole section of ground where the flight of steps is to go, or you can proceed step by step. You need a concrete foundation at the base of the steps, under the first riser, but the other risers may be mortared directly onto a layer of consolidated hardcore. For drainage purposes, the treads must be laid at a slight angle, and a narrow gutter may need to be incorporated.

Retaining walls are really projects for professional builders: earth-moving and shoring equipment will be required; the walls must be anchored and sloped correctly in order to endure the weight of earth behind, which may involve the use of reinforcing rods; and pipes will have to be laid for back drainage and weepholes. In other words, their construction is not to be tackled lightly!

Maintenance of paved areas is largely confined to weed-killing. Some Trust gardens apply a pre-emergent/residual weedkiller like Simazine to paths in early spring, but this is liable to leach into lawn edges and neighbouring borders and cause damage; re-turfing had to be carried out at MONTACUTE as a result of leaching. Simazine should not cause these problems, however, if your paths and top edges are properly constructed – that is, if the lawn is above the level of the paths. A contact weedkiller like Paraquat, which kills the vegetation it touches but leaves no residue in the soil, is preferred by most gardeners. Spraying is carried out two or three times during the growing season.

But if you are environmentally aware and wish to encourage a wealth of wildlife in your garden, you will want to keep the use of chemicals to a minimum. No herbicide of any kind is used at SHEFFIELD PARK; the trampling of the annual 130,000 visitors together with an occasional hoeing in hot weather keeps the weeds away. At GREYS COURT a flame gun is used on the paths. And at SNOWSHILL all the weeding of paved areas is done by hand.

SMOOTH LAWNS AND ROUGH GRASS

A smooth velvet lawn is a traditional feature of the British garden. It is the perfect restful antidote to riotous flower borders and an ideal carpet upon which to set statuary and specimen trees. It is a contrasting colour and texture to other ground covers, mineral and vegetable, and it is pleasantly soft to walk and sit on. Young children can play on it safely, adults can use it for ball games, and dogs can be exercised on it. Indeed, there is no other surface material as visually attractive and as adaptable as grass that is kept short and uniform; and, what is more, a lawn is cheap to install.

Its drawback as a ground cover is that it does require regular attention. Much of this work can be concentrated into a few days at the beginning and end of the season, but mowing at least is a weekly chore. Nevertheless, mowing is accomplished quickly (unless you have rolling acres) and, compared to flower borders and vegetable gardens, rock gardens and rose gardens, a lawn is definitely an easily managed, if not exactly labour-saving, feature.

The purpose of this chapter is not only to show you how to achieve the immaculate lawn but also to show how the work load can be reduced by treating grassed areas in less formal ways. But let me begin on a design note by considering the role of the lawn within the garden's groundplan and its interplay with other features.

An expanse of closely mown lawn plays its traditional role at NYMANS, *Sussex, as an open arena and a foil for plants. A restricted range of flower colours ensures a tranquil scene.*

LAWNS AS DESIGN FEATURES

Lawns provide open spaces, which are necessary as much for aesthetic as for practical reasons. They prevent the garden from seeming claustrophobic and congested; provide pauses for the eye; offer visual access to buildings, countryside and planting compositions; and order their setting. When surrounded by trees, they will also reflect light like a lake.

In town and suburban gardens, the lawn usually occupies the centre of the site and the surrounding vegetation is built up to conceal boundary fences and provide privacy. Many National Trust properties have enclosed gardens or parts of gardens which possess such a central oasis of tranquillity. It may be geometrical or abstract in shape. The walled Mulberry Garden at BATEMAN'S shares a typical rectangular lawn with thousands of private gardens up and down the country; it is divided into two by a straight path and bordered by flowerbeds. A small octagonal lawn is the centrepiece in a gravel arena at the side of PACKWOOD HOUSE. The silent, yew-girdled, green arena in the middle of SISSINGHURST CASTLE'S walled rose garden is circular. And at TRELISSICK a lawn of abstract starfish shape, bounded by numerous trees and bulging rhododendrons and on one side by a wall, is the pool of calm in a garden crammed with horticultural incident; its impact reinforced by its low-lying position (walking downhill relaxes the mind as well as the limbs) and the strategic siting of an inviting bench in the corner.

Lawns which play a static role like this can either be left empty, as voids in the design, or be enlivened. The Mulberry Garden lawn at BATEMAN'S has apple and pear trees as corner posts (mulberries won't grow here!) the main lawn at

A smooth transition from garden to countryside is achieved at HIDCOTE *with the aid of a ha-ha. Evergreen oaks frame the view of Bredon Hill.*

TRELISSICK is dominated by a huge Japanese cedar; and the octagonal lawn at PACKWOOD has a sundial as its pivot. At KNIGHTSHAYES the rectangular lawn of the Old Bowling Green Garden, which is protected by castellated yew hedges, has as its heart a great oval pool; and at SNOWSHILL one of the small lawns supports an ancient wellhead. At BARRINGTON COURT the rectangular lawn in the walled Lily Garden, surrounded by brick paths and colourful herbaceous borders, is interrupted by a pattern of raised flowerbeds as well as by a central pond.

But in the small private garden there may be no place for additional clutter; a straightforward green sward is all that is required. In large gardens, too, the vacant lawn has its place: witness the vast oval lawn at CASTLE DROGO, contained by yew, which is the only occupant of its enclosure; its purpose, as Graham Thomas concludes, to furnish a counterweight to the bulk of the castle nearby, an absence to set against a domineering presence.

If town and suburban gardens tend to be introspective, country gardens tend to be outward-looking. The inspiration for the design usually comes from the nature of the landscape, whose features are welcomed and celebrated. Here there is scope for the lawn to play a truly dynamic role, to pick up the undulations of the ground and to carry the eye over the garden's boundaries to the countryside beyond. Numerous Trust gardens employ a ha-ha to disguise the division between lawn and field; the close-cut grass simply sweeps away from the house and imperceptibly becomes rougher. The intended suggestion is either that the countryside comes right to your back door or that your garden extends over most of the county!

Visually more exciting is the upward sweep to the horizon. At HIDCOTE a long straight grass corridor, flanked by hedges of hornbeam, leads first downhill and then steeply uphill, its focal point and goal being only the open sky at the end. Equally dramatic is the great sloping lawn at POLESDEN LACEY, which climbs vertically to the north and west. On the horizon is a yew hedge which brings the north view to a full

A broad corridor of grass at HIDCOTE takes the eye straight to the horizon. The open gateway at the end promises a reward to those who walk to it.

stop but instead encourages the eye to follow its undulating length uphill to the west. Grass, yew, sky and a glimpse of distant woodland are the composition's only ingredients.

In the enclosed garden the dynamic potential of a lawn can also be harnessed, though the results can never be as breathtaking. Grass can flow around corners and curve around island flowerbeds; or, by means of broad and narrow pathways, it can lead in straight lines. Lawns thus become open channels, directing the course and speed of the eye's route around the site. The planting on either side of the lawn can enhance the effect: curves can be justified by something solid and substantial on their inner edge, and such obstructions help to create mystery and encourage exploration; straight lines can be emphasized by a corresponding line of plants in the adjoining border (a continuous line of irises, for example, or a broken line of slim conifers).

Of course, in large gardens, where short grass is the main form of ground cover, the lawn will continually alternate between being a self-contained arena and a pathway to somewhere else. Although it can often be both simultaneously, the weakest points in the groundplan are usually where it is not immediately clear which role it is playing. Lawns, like all other garden features, need to be consciously planned, for shapeless areas of grass leading off in all directions only make the composition appear restless and incoherent.

The texture, colour and neat uniformity of a grass carpet complements virtually everything it meets. It makes a satisfying contrast to other ground-cover substances – stone, brick, gravel and water, for example – and a sympathetic horizontal plane against which walls, hedges, shrubs and trees can rise. The foliage is so fine that it sets off nearly all other leaves, and although its green hue can be intense, it rarely fights with the colours of flowers. Accordingly, there is nowhere from which, for aesthetic reasons, it has to be banned.

However, practical considerations must influence the way in which gardens are designed, and there are a few locations where grass is unsatisfactory. Firstly, it is not suitable for places that suffer from very heavy traffic. Lawns are hard-wearing but patches that are constantly trampled and compacted quickly turn to mud. Service paths around the house that have to be walked upon daily are obviously better constructed with hard materials. But there will also be junctions in the garden which may take more than their fair share of pounding. Where there is a narrow entrance to a lawn from a patio, or a gateway through which a grass path flows, or where you descend upon grass from a flight of steps, it may be better to substitute a square of brick or stonework. You will see examples of lawns interrupted by small areas of paving in most Trust gardens but I have noticed them particularly at PACKWOOD, where slabs jut out into the lawn in several different spots. One or two slabs may be enough at such junctions; you need not go overboard.

Benches sited on lawns can be advantageously supported and fronted by paving slabs, as at TRELISSICK and MOSELEY OLD HALL; this avoids unattractive scuffing and saves you having to move furniture for mowing. The edge of a lawn that abuts an herbaceous border also benefits from an apron of paving. This is an area that is regularly compacted by feet and often buried by perennials spilling over; gardeners are forced either to clip back offending plants continually, which results in a very self-conscious front line, or to mow around them and expect bare and yellowed patches of lawn in the autumn. What is more, to keep a clean, undented surface, you can only work there by standing on a board to spread your weight and surrounding yourself with sheeting to collect soil and debris. Many Trust gardens now separate their borders from the lawn by means of a narrow strip of paving, even if there was no such detail in the original design. Flowerbeds cut out of lawns are especially labour-intensive, not least because of all the edging work involved.

The eye's progression to the horizon
is leisurely in this HIDCOTE vista, with the change of paving
material, the circle of grass, the steps, the gates and urns, and
the glimpses of flowers and purple foliage beyond.

*Grass banks are fun to walk down but usually less fun
to mow. Banks steeper than this, at* SNOWSHILL, *may be better
given over to low-maintenance ground-cover plants.*

Secondly, grass should not be grown where it is unlikely to thrive. It is unsuitable for use in heavily shaded areas, for example. Here you should make your paths from hard materials, cinders or pulverized bark, and cover your open areas with shade-loving foliage and flowering plants, instead of struggling for a perfect sward with all odds against you. One of the loveliest smooth ground covers for deep shade is moss, which can be established at the expense of other weeds by an occasional spraying with paraquat, but I suspect it is an acquired taste. Alternative treatments should also be sought for excessively damp and excessively dry situations, unless you are prepared to drain or irrigate properly.

Thirdly, grass should be avoided in places that are difficult to mow. Few gardeners are prepared to go to the trouble taken by the staff at POLESDEN LACEY who dangle Flymos on ropes in order to cut the steep grass banks beside the drive. At BODNANT all the slopes in the woodland garden – which are shady as well as precarious to cultivate (the gardeners themselves must be attached to ropes!) – are covered with a form of rush, *Luzula sylvatica*, which grows thickly in both dry and moist positions. It is strimmed once a year, in autumn, to keep it neat and to promote thick sturdy growth. There are all sorts of other ground-cover subjects that can be pressed into service on such tricky sites in place of grass, which will be attractive and labour-saving.

LAWN ESTABLISHMENT AND MAINTENANCE

Some of us inherit lawns, others must make them for ourselves. Time spent on the initial preparation of the ground is always rewarded. Carefully clear the site of rubbish (including tree stumps and roots) and dig down to a spade's depth, loosening the subsoil and turning over the topsoil. Hire a rotovator for large areas. Incorporate some compost or other organic material (several bucketfuls per square yard) and, if the soil is heavy, some grit or river sand. It should not be necessary to alter the pH of the soil, but if conditions are excessively acidic you can apply some lime (70g per square metre / 2oz per square yard); this was done at

Digging down a spade's depth.

Raking the surface until it is level.

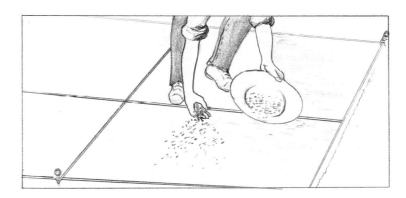

A grid helps to ensure even seed distribution.

LAWN PREPARATION

SHUGBOROUGH recently, on established lawns, with marked results. The ideal pH for lawns is between 5.5 and 6.0; pH meters can now be bought from most garden centres. Then, rake or shallowly rotovate the surface until it is perfectly level and free of clods, and firm it down with either your heels or a roller. Finally, rake again.

This preparation is best carried out during high summer, when the ground is dry. It should then be left to settle for several weeks. September is the ideal month for sowing grass seed, October for turfing; but both operations can be carried out in early April, and the initial preparation undertaken in the autumn. While the ground is fallow, emerging weeds can be controlled with a contact weedkiller. A week before you sow your seed or lay your turf, rake again and scatter some superphosphate fertilizer on the surface in as even a manner as possible.

If the area to be grassed is small and speed is of the essence, turf will be an attractive option. It is satisfying to handle and it gives you an instant lawn.

Make sure that your supplier provides dense-topped,

Place turves in rows. Keep the joints tight and allow some overlap at the end of rows.

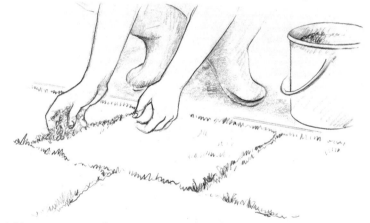

Sprinkle some compost between turves to knit them together and prevent shrinkage.

LAYING A TURF LAWN

rooty turves, of a fairly uniform thickness and ensure that they are free of weeds and coarse grasses. It is a good idea to lay the turves fairly promptly after delivery, but they can be stored for a few days in a shady spot, grass side upwards.

Working forwards from a wooden plank, lay the turves in rows, keeping the joints tight and allowing some overlap at the ends of rows (you can obtain a sharp edge with a half-moon cutter once the lawn is established); use half turves to stagger the cracks, as if you were laying bricks. Sprinkle some soil/compost/sand mixture down the joints to encourage the turves to knit together quickly and to prevent shrinkage. Water the lawn frequently until it is properly settled.

Seeding is a much more economical way of establishing a lawn and the only option for very large areas. It also allows you to choose exactly which combination of grasses you would like to be present. A mixture of Chewing's fescue, creeping red fescue and browntop bent is the perfect mix for an ornamental lawn, and modern varieties of these grasses have been developed which are more compact and require less frequent mowing. For surfaces likely to suffer more than average wear, make sure there is some smooth-stalked meadow grass present. Perennial rye grass is the toughest lawn grass but it is coarse. There are now some newer dwarf varieties of rye grass available which are hard-wearing and fine enough for inclusion in high-quality turf; they are used between the Red Borders and in the Old Garden at HIDCOTE.

To ensure even distribution of seed, divide the area into rows by means of string and pegs, having raked the site first. Then, walking backwards down each row, scatter the seed by hand or by means of a calibrated seed drill at a rate of 50g per square metre / 1½oz per square yard. Finally, rake the ground gently again. Water during dry periods to ensure there is no check on growth and to discourage birds from dust-bathing.

Once there is a sward about 50mm/2in high, lightly roll the surface and give it its first cut on a high setting. Do not apply weedkillers until the lawn is established; remove offending items by hand. Surface irregularities can be remedied by topdressing them with soil/compost/sand.

Lawn maintenance is a topic that greatly occupies the minds of the National Trust gardening staff, for it is usually their most time-consuming task. Careful thought is given to ways of reducing the work load without losing visual perfection. Clearly, modern machinery helps considerably, especially with the task of mowing. Trust outhouses contain an array of machines, each used for a specific purpose. Cylinder mowers (ride-on sorts for large areas, ordinary sorts for small areas) are employed on all areas which need a smooth, formal appearance, usually those nearest to the house. Their scissor-like action gives the neatest finish, and the more blades there are, the finer the results. These are the mowers that provide the best striped effects; stripes not only suggest order but usefully direct the eye.

Rotary mowers are used over the rest of the site, ride-on sorts for most areas and small hover types for banks. They

Stripes can make an interesting addition to the groundplan. In this view from HINTON AMPNER, *Hampshire, they draw the eye to the urn and echo the pattern of the fields beyond.*

can deal with rougher grass (up to a height of 100mm / 4in) and undulating ground, and produce a harder-wearing surface. Strimmers, which usually cut by means of a nylon cord rotating at high speed, are used in the most awkward corners, such as between fence posts, around trees or under shrubs.

The height of the cut has a surprising impact on the intensity of maintenance required. Very close mowing (12mm / ½in or less) can damage root systems and necessitates more feeding and watering; it also encourages the appearance of moss. A cut of 18mm / ¾in not only promotes thicker and tougher growth but reduces the frequency of mowing. Grass clippings are usually removed during the season's early cuts but are left once the speed of growth slows down in summer, except on areas that need a manicured look; in hot weather, grass clippings help to retain moisture. Cylinder mowers have a box for collecting clippings, but those from rotary and hover mowers have to be raked up. Mowing should be carried out with regularity – at ten-day intervals during periods of average growth, and once a week when growth is fast.

Edging is another task that no gardener relishes. At SHUGBOROUGH there are four miles of edges and they are all clipped by hand, for mechanical edging tools tend to scatter the gravel from the paths and are very noisy – disturbance to a garden's tranquillity must always be limited during opening times. But for most of us they certainly help to save time. One means of avoiding the task altogether is to incorporate metal strips or wooden boards, which prevent the grass growing outwards. Plastic edging strips are used at WESTBURY COURT. At FELBRIGG HALL pressure-tanalized deal planks have been inserted into the edges of all the lawns: the turf is rolled back and the planks are positioned just below the level of the lawn and screwed to pegs; soaking the timber enables it to be bent into curves.

But this is expensive and troublesome to undertake. The best solution is to eliminate neat exposed edges from the groundplan, by allowing your lawns to spill over paving, set

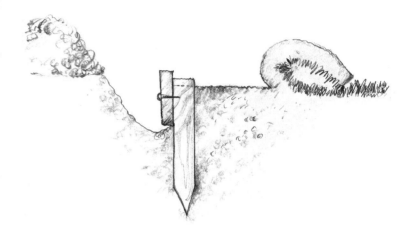

Inserting a wooden edging between the lawn and the path contains the lawn and reduces edging work.

just below the lawn level, to flow under shrubs or to turn into rough grass (see AN ALTERNATIVE PHILOSOPHY below). If you must have edges, and are not prepared to contain them with wood or metal, cut them so that they have a slant downwards and outwards. This stops them collapsing when they are trodden down. Having to edge holes cut out of the lawn for specimen trees (bare soil has to be left around trees until they are established, so that there is no competition for nutrients) can be avoided by filling the holes with bark chippings. Incidentally, oval or diamond-shaped slits, as at KILLERTON, are easier to mow around than squares or circles.

The lawnmower museum at TRERICE, Cornwall, traces the history of the machine's development.

Lawns should not need continual applications of fertilizer, except where the cutting height is low and clippings are removed or where growth is poor because of damage, drought or a naturally thin soil. You will find that if you apply fertilizer to your lawn in generous proportions, you will only have to mow it more frequently as a consequence. When you do have to apply fertilizer, do so sparingly (35g per square metre/1oz per square yard) using a slow-release compound type, applied in early spring when growth has started.

At ANTONY HOUSE, where there are 17 acres of grass to be mown, the formal areas are given a second feed in the autumn; the iron content of this feed helps to toughen the sward and banish red thread disease.

The continual use of mowers and the passage of feet can compact the turf, thus reducing the penetration of water, nutrients and air and causing dead 'thatch' to build up around the grass roots. Aeration can be improved with a fork or an aerating machine. The problem of thatch can similarly be dealt with by hand, using a rake to pull out the debris, or by a machine. The latter is, of course easier. Carry out the job in September with a powered scarifier, which can be hired for the occasion. After aerating or scarifying, topdress with a soil/compost/sand mixture to which a little slow-release fertilizer has been added.

Weeds and moss ought not to be a serious problem on fertile lawns that are regularly mown, aerated and scarified. Individual weeds, such as dandelions or plantain, can be dug out with a thin trowel or treated with spot weedkillers. Neat salt is used to kill dandelions at SNOWSHILL. For more extensive infestations you can apply a selective herbicide. Combined herbicides and granular fertilizers are also available. Moss can be controlled with lawn sand or mosskiller

and, on very acid soils, with a sprinkling of lime (70g per square metre/2oz per square yard). Spring scarification is undertaken at WALLINGTON to remove moss after wet winters.

Neglected lawns usually respond quickly to good management but occasionally you may feel that a more drastic remedy is required. Such was recently practised at BODNANT, where the formal lawns were suffering badly from compaction caused by the large number of visitors and were being progressively choked by moss and daisies. The Head Gardener, Mr Martin Puddle, took the bull by the horns in the summer of 1984 and with the help of contractors carried out a programme of renovation. Firstly, mosskiller was applied using a knapsack sprayer with a 1.2m/4ft boom (conditions were windy, so pieces of chipboard were used as barriers to prevent the spray drifting into the lily pond). Five days later the moss was dead and the lawns were scarified three ways and swept by machine. A slit-tining machine was then employed (this aerates by removing narrow cylindrical plugs of earth at regular intervals) and the area was over-seeded by direct drill seeder, using a mixture of compact, hard-wearing browntop bent, Chewing's fescue and dwarf creeping red fescue. Some fertilizer was later applied to encourage root growth. The results have been highly satisfactory, and repetition of this procedure will be carried out on a smaller scale at periodic intervals.

GRASS – AN ALTERNATIVE PHILOSOPHY

Unless a manicured appearance is absolutely essential for reasons of design or practicality, there is no need for gardeners to strive for the perfect lawn. Indeed, a more relaxed attitude to grassed areas suits modern gardening particularly well, for it not only leads to a lightened work load but also to a more natural garden, less dependent on chemicals and more varied in its native flora.

The use of weedkillers has been discontinued in many Trust gardens, even on closely mown lawns. Clover and speedwell have been permitted to colonize at SNOWSHILL, for example; daisies seed themselves at BATEMAN's; and the main lawn at POLESDEN LACEY is threaded with creeping thyme and turns quite red at flowering time.

In less formal areas, grass is allowed to grow taller and mowing is carried out less frequently. A smooth lawn may have to be cut thirty times a year, but if the length of sward is maintained at 100mm/4in instead of 18mm/¾in the mowing frequency is reduced to about fourteen times, and represents an enormous saving of labour. You can cut at any intermediate height you like, simply choosing that which is the best compromise in terms of visual appearance and maintenance commitment. At SHUGBOROUGH all grass, outside the main formal areas, is cut at 45mm/1⅞in. At KNIGHTSHAYES it is cut at 60mm/2½in; mowing begins at the end of June and is done every eight or nine days thereafter. And at TRELISSICK it is cut at 85mm/3½in. Rotary mowers are usually employed on medium-height grass, large flail mowers on very rough areas. Grass clippings are left. Feeding is rarely necessary but on very thin ground, as at ANTONY HOUSE, a fertilizer may be applied every five years.

Leaving part of the garden rough and part close-cut often helps to strike the right balance, and can be a pleasing element in the design. At GREYS COURT the ground rises in tiers behind the house and as it does so, the grass changes from fine lawn, to medium-mown turf, to coarse field, making a splendid visual transition. Before the advent of the lawn-mower many gardens would have looked like this; the Pleasure Ground, often around the house, would have been hand mown with a scythe, the Inner Park grazed by sheep and the Outer Park grazed by cattle or deer. But the join between rough and smooth can also be abrupt, as at STOURHEAD, where the curved line of rough turf at the end of the main lawn marks a definite frontier in the design and signals a change of mood; the sweep follows the undulations of the ground and is a dynamic statement. Incidentally, you can also use a change of grass height to direct the feet; no one will walk straight out on to rough turf if they are enticed in another direction by smooth lawn. At STOURHEAD you are encouraged to turn to the side and rejoin the footpath.

A close-mown path through a rough wild-flower meadow.

Closely mown grass paths can also be channelled through areas of rougher grass. These can wind and meander or follow straight lines, depending on whether you want an informal or formal effect. Or patches of rough grass can simply be left as islands within the lawn, perhaps around the boles of mature trees or on bits of ground that are awkward to cut.

It is only a short step from deciding to have different heights of grass to deciding to have plants growing in it. But before I explore the subject of wildflower gardening, let me take the flower borders to that point too, for they also may be treated in varying degrees of informality.

GROUND-COVER PLANTING

The term ground-cover planting earned itself a bad name in the 1970s when it became synonymous with drab uniformity. Every overworked municipal council and lazy home gardener embraced the concept with glee and the result was interminable borders of St John's wort, heather, periwinkle, and Irish ivy, a sea of dusty greenery pleasing only to woodlice. In fact every form of gardening is open to mismanagement and it would be just as ludicrous to dismiss ground-cover planting because of the aberrations of 1970s fashion as it would be to forbid the bedding-out of annuals and biennials because of Victorian bad taste. Ground-cover planting has an important place in today's garden and it can be among the most rewarding of treatments.

I suppose a definition of ground-cover planting would be the establishment of a permanent dense layer of vegetation which suppresses weeds and minimizes labour. The idea is to make a self-sufficient plant community in which plants happily co-exist more or less as they do in nature. And what a blissful idea it is to have a garden organized so that its owner can spend most of his time musing and pottering and dreaming up new projects instead of being forever saddled with repetitive chores. Even the National Trust with its permanent gardening staff is always looking for ways to keep costs down by reducing work and making the best use of the gardeners' time, and its gardens contain numerous examples of labour-saving planting. With certain areas requiring only minimal maintenance, gardeners can lavish more attention on the labour-intensive herbaceous borders and rose gardens, fruit trees and topiary.

Suitable plants for participating in ground-cover schemes range widely from sizeable shrubs like azaleas and laurels – which clothe themselves in leaves right to the ground and occupy a fair amount of ground space – and thicket-forming bamboos, to low perennials like bergenias, comfreys and hardy geraniums which either form impenetrable clumps or spread to make closely woven carpets. In fact, any plant which is strong (i.e. does not take bullying by neighbours), is self-reliant (does not need staking or otherwise cosseting) and grows thickly is a candidate for a ground-cover scheme.

What distinguishes the winners is their year-round presentability. Attractive foliage is obviously the key asset, and if this is evergreen too, so much the better. The longer the leaves are present, the less likely it is that weeds will find the light and elbow room to establish themselves. Many of the best ground-cover subjects also give an eyecatching display of flowers in season, so there is no need to deprive yourself of ephemeral colour, but it is the shapes, sizes and textures of the foliage, and the relative heights of the plants, which ultimately determine how they are used and juxtaposed.

STYLE AND PHILOSOPHY

In design terms, ground-cover planting is a halfway house between the contrived and the natural. Schemes do not

A colourful display of bank planting at BODNANT, Gwynedd, combining azaleas, laurels and rhododendrons.

Lamb's ears (Stachys byzantina)

to just one variety, though, or you will spoil the structural effect. Which variety you select depends upon the height, shape and texture that is best for the design.

The bank of hypericum at CLEVEDON COURT, the twin beds of *Euonymus* 'Emerald Gaiety' flanking steps at STOURHEAD and even the rows of lavender on the terraces at SHUGBOROUGH are examples of ground covers used in formal linear ways. At BODNANT liriope and epimedium are employed as edging strips to borders, catmint fringes the borders at BATEMAN'S and at POLESDEN LACEY male ferns create a ribbon of greenery in front of yews. *Geranium macrorrhizum*, green and black ophiopogon, *Stachys byzantina (S. lanata)*, pachysandra and *Iris foetidissima* are also neat and uniform enough for this job. Perhaps the most successful candidate for low formal work is bergenia. Dense, chunky and evergreen, it can play a proper sculptural role at the edge or corner of a border, and is especially good against stone and brick, as at CHARLECOTE.

Geometrical beds that have been cut out of grass or which abut paved areas will have their formal shapes reinforced if they are filled with just one variety of plant. The two circular beds of catmint around the stone urns on the lower terrace at KNIGHTSHAYES help to provide a last humanizing touch before the lawn slips over the ha-ha into the countryside beyond. At BUSCOT a circular sunken arena forms the pivot for straight avenues of poplars and fastigiate oaks. It has as its centrepiece a stone wellhead. The approach to the arena is via grass, and indeed its sloped sides are also of grass (flymown once a month), but the middle has been filled with feathery junipers – a medium-sized variety with ascending branches called 'Grey Owl'. The effect is of swirling mist softening the hard vertical and horizontal lines of the trees, wellhead and grass.

proclaim themselves to be triumphantly man-made, like immaculately graded herbaceous borders or manicured rose gardens, but neither are they coarse and wild enough to be mistaken for nature's handiwork. As in the wild, the plant community knits together to conceal every trace of bare earth; but, as in the contrived border, the ingredients have been selected for their visual impact and associated for colour and foliage effect.

How you choose and use your plants determines whether man or nature appears to have the upper hand. Around the house you may want quite a formal effect, to plant in straight lines to emphasize a symmetrical groundplan or to fill square or circular beds with uniform vegetation. Ground-cover plants can undertake this formalizing role. Restrict yourself

This run of 'Hidcote' lavender at
MOTTISFONT ABBEY, Hampshire, is an example of formal
ground-cover planting. It lends an additional colour and texture
(and scent) without disturbing the simplicity of the design or
vying for attention with the statue.

Such treatments are easily reduced in scale for the average small garden. Specimen trees can be grown in a circle, square or diamond of ground cover in the lawn, for example. A friend of mine has a white-stemmed birch in a pool of purple-leaved *Viola labradorica*. But often the size and shape of beds you encounter in Trust gardens will correspond exactly to your own. The small triangular bed beside the entrance path at TRELISSICK, carpeted with the white-flowered *Lamium maculatum album*, the square beds of silver *Stachys byzantina*, golden marjoram and black-leaved ophiopogon under the apple and pear trees at POWIS CASTLE, or those on the gravel terrace at MONTACUTE, stuffed with yuccas, provide ideas on a readily identifiable scale.

It is true to say that any ground-cover plant used *en masse* will, to a greater or lesser extent, formalize the scene. Mother Nature does not plant in neat blocks. But by introducing more than one variety of plant, or by choosing a plant that does not grow in a tidy uniform manner, and by allowing the groups to form irregular drifts within the bed, a more relaxed air is created. Thus an island bed in the lawn comprising bulging shrub roses underplanted with various hardy geraniums, as at KNIGHTSHAYES, or a vast unpredictable wave of tall frothy *Polygonum campanulatum* (now *Persicaria campanulata)*, with pink flowerheads, which surges between trees and shrubs, as at NYMANS, looks far less contrived.

Still more informal is to reduce the size of the plant groups and introduce even greater variety. A non-geometrical shape to the bed helps to some degree, but not as much as most novice gardeners might think; it is the planting that usually sets the tone. A sweep of one plant meets a slightly shorter or longer sweep of another plant and such encounters are repeated, using a number of different plant varieties, throughout the bed. In broad areas the foreground is occupied by herbaceous perennials and low shrubs, and the background by larger shrubs; but here and there the tiered effect is interrupted by a tree or by a tall shrub coming forward. In narrow borders the undulations are from side to side instead of from front to back.

Examples abound in Trust gardens as this is the most common approach to ground-cover planting. The woodland connections of rhododendrons, azaleas and hydrangeas, fronted by ferns, skimmias and vacciniums, the streamside beds of bamboos, hostas, gunneras, *Iris sibirica* and astilbes, the rockery banks of conifers, prostrate polygonums and heathers, and the sunny borders of senecios, hebes and sages interplanted with sedums, stachys and helianthemums are all intended to be labour-saving schemes.

The skill lies in selecting ingredients that will thrive under the conditions available and yet will not be so lusty as to threaten their neighbours. Vigorous plants which spread by underground runners or surface-rooting stems are largely omitted from mixed beds; where these excel is in isolation on difficult sites among established trees and shrubs. Ideal plants are those which expand sideways progressively and uniformly – clump-forming perennials and mound-forming shrubs.

In such ground-cover plantings each ingredient has its own territory, and demarcation lines are clearly defined, even though neighbours may appear to blend into one another. What you are creating are thus simply labour-saving versions of ordinary ornamental borders, and they can look just as presentable and appropriate close to the house, adjoining a mown lawn or patio, as on a boundary line with the countryside.

The last stage of informality that ground-cover planting can reach before it turns into wild gardening is where there is total integration between neighbours. Here, instead of arranging that one plant stops where another plant starts, you encourage interweaving and self-seeding. A complete hotchpotch is prevented because you match plants of equal

Trees and shrubs can be used to break the
flow of the grass and help to integrate the lawn with
the planted areas. They can also be useful for blocking views.
An American buckeye (Aesculus pavia) has been planted
as a lawn specimen at ACORN BANK, Cumbria.

vigour, seek out attractive varieties that will be mutually complimentary in colour and form, and again avoid the real tyrants. It is not really wild gardening because you are still working with garden plants within delineated borders, but the effects certainly seem totally uncontrived.

The supreme example of a garden displaying this type of planting is STANDEN. This 12-acre garden is managed by just one full-time gardener and is a treasure trove of labour-saving ideas. The meandering gravel paths are bordered by sloping banks smothered in a complex tapestry of ground-cover plants. Bergenias, ivies, cotoneasters, hebes, *Polygonum vacciniifolium* (now *Persicaria vacciniifolia*), epimediums, tellima and heathers plot and conspire against each other, while ferns and *Iris foetidissima* stand sentinel among them. But, though every plant is forever behind enemy lines, none ever seems to win a battle outright.

PLANTING IDEAS

Whichever style of planting you opt for, your choice of plant material is governed by the nature of your soil and the amount of sunlight enjoyed. Once you know whether you are on acid, neutral or alkaline ground, and whether it is free-draining, averagely retentive or boggy, you can let yourself be guided by the quality of the illumination that each bed receives.

Some ground-cover plants seem to grow equally well in sun, part shade and shade (polygonum, trachystemon, *Geranium macrorrhizum*, Japanese anemones, London pride, ivy, climbing hydrangea, *Rubus tricolor*, hypericum and euonymus, for example) but most have a preference. The art is to select varieties that will succeed under the conditions on offer, that will be appropriate in mood, and that will make a long-lasting contribution.

At STANDEN, Sussex, ground-cover plants are used on a large scale. They are grown informally and encouraged to mingle. Here Geranium 'Johnson's Blue' billows under an indigofera, and rhododendrons take up the colour beyond the lawn.

A sunny corner at MOTTISFONT ABBEY, *Hampshire is carpeted by purple sage,* Stachys lanata *and* Geranium *'Mavis Simpson'.*

The Sunny Border

Sunny borders are perhaps the most desirable habitats in the garden, especially if they benefit from some shelter. They are the places in which the majority of those colourful summer-flowering perennials and shrubs perform best and where gardeners most like to potter. Yet even here there may be a need to reduce work by employing ground-cover ingredients.

On the gravel parterre at KILLERTON is a series of stone-edged rectangular beds which have been filled entirely with low-maintenance plants. When I went there in spring everything seemed neatly contained, for the ingredients are cut back annually, but by my next visit in high summer, things were happily overflowing on to the paths and cascading into one another and had created a mat of vegetation quite impenetrable to weeds. The combination of the formal groundplan, complete with Coade stone vases, and the totally informal plant community was highly effective. The cushion and duvet shapes are provided by catmint, santolina, senecio, helianthemum, fuchsia and hypericum, the vertical accents by yuccas.

Many of the best ground-cover plants for such low to mid-height sunny schemes are the silvery or aromatic shrubs and sub-shrubs from the Mediterranean region – the lavenders, cistuses, rosemaries, sages, phlomis, thymes, rues, ballotas and hyssops. They are highly compatible and make evocative hummocky combinations for gardens that are not excessively cold or wet. To provide contrasting greens and stimulating juxtapositions of form add potentillas, hebes, dwarf brooms, acanthus, euphorbias, sedums, *Iris innominata, I. graminea* and calamintha. If your garden is quite cold, use these as your mainstays.

A similar pattern of beds to that at KILLERTON, but on a smaller scale, is found in the little Paved Garden at KNIGHTS-HAYES. Again we have a formal groundplan, its focal point being a huge lead tank supported on a dais, but here the planting is kept symmetrical, low and neat. At one end a pair of beds is filled with germander (*Teucrium chamaedrys*); at the other end with rock-garden geraniums, magenta *G. sanguineum* and its pale pink variety *G. s. striatum*, interspersed with *Allium karataviense*. The middle four beds contain violet *Campanula portenschlagiana* and silver-leaved artemisia (the artemisias are protected from excess damp during the winter by glass cloches, but this would not be necessary on light soil; if you are worried, grow *Cerastium tomentosum columnae* or *Anaphalis triplinervis* instead).

Most of the plants used here would normally be found in rock gardens. Because rock gardening is associated with hard work in most people's mind, this category of plant does not immediately occur to gardeners planning labour-saving borders. But certain hearty subjects lend themselves well as ground cover, and can be used on the flat or on sunny banks. Other contenders include acaena, *Campanula carpatica*, *C. alliariifolia*, *C. latiloba*, dianthus, erigeron, geum, *Phlox amoena*, *P. douglasii*, *P. stolonifera*, *P. subulata*, waldsteinia, zauschneria, ceratostigma, *Veronica gentianoides*, *V. spicata incana*, arabis, armeria, ajuga and alyssum. Beware of invasive cotula and saponaria, and avoid at all costs the ineradicable *Campanula rapunculoides*.

In the small Laundry Court at MONTACUTE there is no soil visible in the perimeter borders, which are crammed with ground-cover plants of varying textures. Large clumps of bergenia, *Stachys byzantina*, *Alchemilla mollis*, *Viola cornuta lilacina*, *Geranium himalayense*, *G. 'Johnson's Blue'* and doronicum provide the living carpet; all these low-growing perennials are easy on any soil in sun or part shade, except for the stachys which likes good light and reasonable drainage.

The geraniums in particular are invaluable constituents and the various species and cultivars display a range of pink, violet, purple and white flowers. Most bloom in late spring and early summer, but some are perpetual-flowering (notably pink *G. endressii* and its cultivars, violet *G. 'Johnson's Blue'* and *G. himalayense*) and some have foliage which takes on rich crimson tints in autumn (*G. macrorrhizum* and its

Bergenia cordifolia

Detail of Geranium *'Johnson's Blue' at* STANDEN.

cultivars). *Viola cornuta* blooms all summer and only needs to be cut back in the autumn; the species, which is violet, and its white variant, *V. c. alba,* are easily raised from seed, but named forms like pale *V. c. lilacina* will have to be bought as divisions or cuttings. Alchemilla makes a delightful haze of lime green when in flower and its hairy scalloped leaves excel at capturing raindrops; but you must remember to shave it to the ground before the flowerheads turn brown in July, or you will be knee-deep in seedlings.

These perennials can be used in the open or beneath and between large sun-loving shrubs, where they will not object to dappled shade. They are obvious companions for shrub roses, among which the best for labour-saving schemes are probably forms and hybrids of *Rosa rugosa.* These are problem-free, have lush green foliage, give a long display of highly scented flowers, in shades of magenta-crimson, pink and white, and as a finale the single-flowered varieties bury themselves in plump hips. After the first year, when they should be cut back hard, they will need no regular pruning, other than the removal of dead or weak stems.

By underplanting with carpeting perennials you can make use of a wide selection of shrubs in your ground-cover schemes. Even subjects that are quite light in growth can be incorporated. At SALTRAM buddleia and *Syringa × josiflexa* 'Bellicent', that delectable lilac with loose plumes of drooping pink funnels, grow in a lake of *Vinca minor;* neither of these shrubs is dense but the periwinkle takes care of the weed problem. At DUNSTER buddleia is underplanted with a sizeable weed-smothering shrub, *Senecio* (now *Brachyglotis*) 'Sunshine'.

Denser shrubs, once mature, will need little assistance in covering the ground. Groups of philadelphus, berberis, rhododendron and photinia, like those in the High Garden at LANHYDROCK, clumps of massive-leaved *Viburnum rhytidophyllum,* as at POLESDEN LACEY, or umbrella stands of Japanese maples, as at COTEHELE, leave little light for interlopers. Some shrubs, however, are clearly better cut out for this work than others. Solid evergreens like *Prunus*

laurocerasus 'Otto Luyken', *Viburnum davidii* and skimmia (all of which grow equally well in shade), spreading and prostrate junipers, and mound- and hummock-forming deciduous shrubs like *Cotoneaster horizontalis* and *Berberis thunbergii* are excellent. But perhaps the most exciting of the frontrunners are *Viburnum plicatum* and its cultivars. Apart from fulfilling their practical obligations they make a real contribution to the seasonal drama, for their horizontal tiers are studded with huge white lacecap flowers in early summer and turn from green to deepest plum-red in autumn. At GLENDURGAN *V. p.* 'Lanarth' takes control of dozens of square feet of rough ground in the dell and is eyecatching even in a setting full of horticultural distraction.

Banks and Sloping Sites

There are two categories of plant whose virtues I have not yet extolled but which are classic ground-cover subjects for sunny areas: conifers and heathers. Both need careful placing. They are so evocative of rugged scenery, of mountainside, cavernous forest and moorland, that they can easily look out of place in gardens riotous with lush woodland and meadow plants. Tight compact conifers can be readily accommodated if they are treated as architectural adjuncts in the garden's design – yew and hemlock walls, juniper pillars etc – and so can coniferous trees which stand above the colourful mêlée and do not participate directly, but feathery cypresses and skeletal pines and the general run of ornamental conifers should be treated with circumspection. Heathers are even trickier to use.

If you do not happen to live in the sort of landscape where conifers and heathers seem natural inhabitants, choose spots for them within your garden where they can be isolated. The most appropriate locations are rock gardens, banks and slopes. Mounds of low *Juniperus procumbens, J. horizontalis* and *J. sabina* 'Tamariscifolia' are most effective when flowing down a formal bank in place of grass; and the larger *J. × media* is also splendid here, especially beside stone steps. Huge prostrate *J. × m.* 'Pfitzeriana' mark the corners of the

Climbing and rambler roses can make good ground-cover plants, especially on banks. 'Sanders' White' arches over the ground at MOTTISFONT ABBEY, *Hampshire, between flax and* Allium christophii.

main terrace at KNIGHTSHAYES, disguising the points where rigid formality meets natural undulation. Sprawling conifers are particularly adept at concealing such weak points in the groundplan and harmonizing disparate materials or treatments.

Juniperus sabina and *J.* × *media* cultivars thrive in shady as well as sunny sites, but the majority of conifers like plenty of light. Heathers are definitely sun-lovers. They are used with conifers and other shrubs on gently sloping ground at WAKEHURST PLACE, growing in island beds cut out of the lawn (they are treated similarly at NYMANS and the Royal Horticultural Society's garden at Wisley), but the hilltop setting they are given at BODNANT demonstrates their true place in the garden – in open exposed sites, away from grass and among rocks.

The Heather Garden at BODNANT, begun only in 1986, is located at the highest point in the garden (the gardeners call it 'K2'!); it is windswept and the soil is poor and shallow, though this has now been considerably improved with the addition of peat and leaf-mould. Although backed by Monterey pines *(Pinus radiata),* and interspersed with the odd conifer to give height here and there, the composition revolves entirely around its rocky outcrops and its heathers, which have been selected for all-year flower and foliage effect.

Among the best heathers for foliage colour are *Calluna vulgaris* 'Golden Carpet' (gold in summer/red in winter), *C. v.* 'Robert Chapman' (gold/red/yellow), *C. v.* 'Silver Queen' (silver grey), *Erica carnea* 'Ann Sparkes' (orange/red) and *E.* × *darleyensis* 'Jack H. Brummage' (yellow). Among the best for flower colour are *Calluna vulgaris* 'Allegro' (dark red in late summer), *C. v.* 'H. E. Beale' (double pink in autumn), *Erica carnea* 'King George' (rose-pink in winter), *E. c.* 'Springwood White' (white in late winter), *E. cinerea* 'Velvet Knight' (plum in summer), *E.* × *darleyensis* 'Darley Dale' (pink in winter and spring), *E. erigena* 'W. T. Rackliff' (white in spring) and the *E. vagans* cultivars 'Cream', 'Mrs D. F. Maxwell' (cerise) and 'St Keverne' (salmon) which bloom in

late summer and autumn. My own favourites are the *E. tetralix* heathers with their silver-grey foliage and pink or white flowers in summer: 'Alba Mollis' (white), 'Ken Underwood' (rose), 'Pink Star' (bright pink) and 'Hookstone Pink' (pale pink). The calluna and daboecia heathers, together with *Erica cinerea, E. tetralix* and *E. vagans*, really need a lime-free soil; *E. arborea, E. carnea* and *E. erigena* will grow on all soils.

Conifers and heathers are not only the ground-cover plants for banks and slopes. DUNSTER CASTLE is a showcase of alternatives. The rocky outcrop on which the castle is perched is festooned with an array of carpeting shrubs and perennials planted in massive groups. Hydrangeas, laurels, senecio, leycesteria, yew, *Lonicera syringantha, Lamium galeobdolon*, ivy, Rubus tricolor, periwinkle and those seaside favourites escallonia and fuchsia divide the ground between them. I have never seen ground-cover plantings on such a scale before.

Many other Trust properties use ground cover on banks – these are, after all, some of the most awkward areas to mow or weed – so planting ideas are numerous. Except in areas of high rainfall, the most suitable plants are likely to be those sun or shade-loving subjects which can tolerate some drought, for here water drains away quickly. In sun, the front-runners are conifers, heathers, bergenias, acanthus, cotoneasters, hebes and mat-forming rock plants like aubrieta, cerastium and helianthemum; in shade, euonymus, gaultheria, ivy, periwinkle, pachysandra, rubus, hypericum, *Euphorbia amygdaloides robbiae* and *Lamium galeobdolon*.

OPPOSITE: *A labour-saving bed of heathers, camellias and other shrubs provides winter colour at* WAKEHURST PLACE, *Sussex.*

FOLLOWING PAGES: *The dense foliage of many rhododendrons and azaleas gives little opportunity for weeds to infiltrate. A native rush,* Luzula sylvatica, *is encouraged to colonize the open spaces on these steep banks at* BODNANT, *North Wales.*

A weed-suppressing carpet of Polygonum affine *'Superbum' (now* Persicaria affinis *'Superba') makes a stunning late summer feature at* WAKEHURST PLACE.

But one is always encountering more exciting subjects. In the mild climate of CLEVEDON COURT, *Ceanothus* 'Cascade' makes a sheet of light blue on the bank below the famous terrace, whose original planting by Shirley Hibberd was ridiculed by Gertrude Jekyll. At KNIGHTSHAYES pink *Clematis montana rubens* flows beside steps (not many gardeners think of using climbers as ground cover, but banks are an obvious place for their trailing stems). At KILLERTON the unusual half-hardy *Hypericum × moserianum* covers a sloping bank in front of the Bear Hut and is shaved to the ground every spring to make way for the lily-of-the-valley with which it is underplanted (another bank at KILLERTON is a thicket of snowberry bushes, whose stems are removed every two years to be turned into besoms: much better than birch apparently!) But I am most covetous of the bank of *Polygonum affine* 'Superbum' (now *Persicaria affinis* 'Superba') beside the waterfall at WAKEHURST PLACE, whose little bottle-brushes – some white and some crimson-red – make a stunning bicoloured display for several months during the summer and autumn.

The Shady Border
Sunless areas of the garden are invariably regarded by novice gardeners as problem sites. In fact they are just as easy to populate with plants as sunny areas, providing you identify the type of shade you are dealing with and select your ingredients accordingly. For our present purpose, I think it is enough to distinguish between open shade (north- and east-facing borders and woodland clearings, where there is little direct sunlight but no overhead canopy of leaves), dappled shade (areas underneath deciduous trees and large shrubs, which are open to the sun during the winter and receive filtered light for the rest of the year) and full shade (areas underneath evergreen or dense deciduous trees and shrubs which are very dark for all or most of the year).

In open shade, it is possible to pursue a range of ground-cover treatments. You can plant great blocks or lines of individual plants – a hosta border, perhaps, such as that at

LANHYDROCK (here the border is in sun, for the soil is retentive enough to keep their flabby foliage turgid; shade is a safer place in most gardens); a hydrangea or fuchsia border such as those at BODNANT, where you could grow a mixture of hardy varieties or confine yourself to just one; or a day-lily border such as those at ANTONY HOUSE (there are 500 varieties here!).

You can forge simple partnerships between plants of varying heights, colours and seasons of interest – the pale yellow, winter-flowering witch-hazel *Hamamelis japonica* 'Zuccariniana' with blue spring-flowering *Symphytum caucasicum*, as at KILLERTON; *Geranium macrorrhizum* interplanted with magenta *G. procurrens*, which performs several months after its bedfellow, as on a bank at POWIS CASTLE (the latter is invasive but a huge bed of it, as at STANDEN, is exceedingly beautiful); or *Helleborus orientalis* hybrids with fuchsias and pink and white Japanese anemones (a scheme which provides colour for most of the year), as at SNOWSHILL.

Or you can opt for more complex schemes employing a quantity of billowing shrubs and carpeting perennials. There is no shortage of candidates as almost every shade-loving plant will thrive in open shade, the only exceptions being those half-hardy subjects or early performers which receive valuable frost protection from an overhead canopy. Aucuba, chaenomeles (the familiar 'japonica' or flowering quince), cotoneaster, euonymus, forsythia, hydrangea, hypericum, mahonia, pachysandra, rhododendron, rubus, sarcococca, skimmia, *Viburnum davidii* and *V. tinus* and vinca, are likely to be your mainstays among shrubs; ajuga, alchemilla, anemone, aruncus, astrantia, brunnera, epimedium, *Euphorbia amygdaloides robbiae,* geranium, helleborus, hemerocallis, heuchera, hosta, *Iris foetidissima*, lamium, omphalodes, pulmonaria, saxifraga (especially London pride), symphytum, tellima, tiarella and waldsteinia among perennials.

The list of plants for dappled shade is more or less identical, but you do not have *carte blanche* in their selection. You have to let yourself be governed by the height and density of the canopy above them. Under very tall trees

Lesser periwinkle (Vinca minor)

Flowering quince (Chaenomeles japonica)

which allow plenty of sunlight through their tracery of leaves and branches, there is room to introduce two layers of vegetation in the form of large shrubs underplanted with perennials, small shrubs and bulbs, exactly as we can do in open positions. But where the canopy is low or relatively dense, you must confine yourself to short ingredients.

You can plant dappled shade formally: the avenue of pleached hornbeam at BUSCOT, for example, is underplanted with straight rows of day-lilies with *Allium christophii (A. albopilosum)* among them; or informally: under the pear arch at BATEMAN'S is a mixed community including clumps of liriope, geraniums, epimedium, *Viola labradorica* 'Purpurea', brunnera, vinca, tiarella, lily-of-the-valley and cyclamen. But when there is a large empty bed beneath trees the opportunity of conjuring up an enchanted woodland with loose groups of shrubs and pools of perennials should never be missed.

KNIGHTSHAYES has just such a woodland and it not only demonstrates planting schemes for all types of shade, but it also shows how exciting ground-cover planting can be when the ingredients are mixed with an artist's eye. A wonderful tan-coloured scheme centres on a rusty-trunked birch, *Betula ermanii* var. *subcordata*, whose light foliage shades a specimen of *Rhododendron falconeri*, which has trusses of cream flowers and brown suede undersides to its leaves, and a great carpet of the tan-flushed creeping fern *Blechnum penna-marina*. Mats of oriental hellebores are spread under magnolias, *Euonymus planipes (E. sachalinensis)* and white-variegated aralia; acid-green euphorbias and bluebells swirl around the skirts of white snowball shrubs, *Viburnum opulus* 'Roseum' (*V. o.* 'Sterile'). Bowles's golden grass combines with electric-blue *Omphalodes cappadocica*; purple-leaved violas with pale blue anemones; and yellow-flowered

Irish ivy is the traditional standby for those heavily shaded, dry areas where nothing else seems to grow, including grass. Here it thrives under cedars at ANGLESEY ABBEY, *Cambridgeshire.*

Lamium galeobdolon with orange *Euphorbia griffithii* 'Fireglow'. Martagon lilies, foxgloves and Solomon's seal provide vertical accents; bulbs pop up unexpectedly (dark blue camassias among pink geraniums, pale wood anemones among dark ajuga); and everywhere there are ferns. One comes away drunk with ideas; if only the labelling was better!

Full shade provides far less scope for plantsmanship. No plants will grow in total darkness and only a few will tolerate long periods of gloom, especially when, as is usually the case, this is accompanied by very dry soil. In the deep shade of dense deciduous trees, such as chestnuts and beeches, two categories of plant are best equipped to succeed; early-flowering bulbs and drought-tolerant evergreens. Snowdrops, *Crocus tommasinianus*, wood anemones, cyclamen, *Scilla mischtschenkoana (S. tubergeniana)* and winter aconites are the outstanding examples of bulbs whose cycle coincides nicely with leafless trees – so they have light and water while they are active, and which do not object to drought thereafter. Evergreen companions for them include holly, box, *Lonicera pileata*, laurel, aucuba, gaultheria, ivy, pachysandra, *Rubus tricolor*, sarcococca, vinca, *Ruscus aculeatus, Iris foetidissima*, lamium including *L. galeobdolon, Symphytum grandiflorum* and waldsteinia.

If your soil is quite retentive you can be more adventurous in your choice of subject. At KNIGHTSHAYES and KILLERTON, Pacific Coast irises thrive and form stout clumps in surprisingly shady conditions close to tree trunks. These are evergreen, June-flowering irises which come in a range of colours from violet to biscuit-brown.

The unpretentious, rustic atmosphere of SNOWSHILL MANOR *garden is achieved by using native and near-native plants and encouraging wildflowers to colonize. The grass under the avenue of guelder roses is home to scillas and celandine.*

You cannot plant directly under evergreen trees unless there is some illumination. If the trees have low leaf cover you can either turn your back on the site and leave the soil bare – weeds will not attempt colonization here – or remove some lower branches to allow light in. Such deeply shaded habitats can support the toughest of the evergreens in the above list. Irish ivy (*Hedera helix* 'Hibernica'), ruscus, *Vinca minor*, rubus and gaultheria are probably the frontrunners. But this is not a suitable habitat for bulbs.

Under the edges of bulky evergreen trees, however, or under very tall bare ones (such as mature pines) there will be enough light for a fuller range of evergreen underplanting; but the soil is still likely to be excessively dry, so choose accordingly. Cyclamen are usually successful around the boles of pines, particularly if they are cosseted occasionally with leaf-mould, and at KNIGHTSHAYES *Viola labradorica* 'Purpurea' grows here, too. Waldsteinia laps a yew hedge at BATEMAN'S, making a thick formal cover but not producing flowers (variegated *Vinca minor* plays this role at POLESDEN LACEY; plain *Vinca minor* at CHARLECOTE), and on the sunny side of a pair of yew pillars, *Geranium renardii* is also pressed reluctantly into service. CHARLECOTE has a stunning association in a small square bed under a thinly clothed yew: a prostrate creamy yellow ivy, *Hedera colchica* 'Dentata Variegata', pierced by sheaves of mauve *Colchicum tenorei*.

Streamsides and Boggy Sites

Damp ground is often awkward and unpleasant to maintain and is one of the places most appropriate for ground-cover treatment. Large clumps of lush perennials are the mainstay of such schemes, interspersed with groups of moisture-loving shrubs like willows, elders and dogwoods. *Gunnera manicata* is the king of the swamp, but its hairy leaves are so enormous that they can easily upset the scale of compositions. Many big Trust gardens give it a home and there is an impressive stand of it in a ditch at NYMANS under the hardy palm *Trachycarpus fortunei*. But in small gardens it is better to use the ornamental rhubarbs (rheum) as substitutes. Their

red young foliage and developing flower spikes are a delight to watch in spring, and the umbrellas of greenery are powerfully architectural.

Hostas provide the bog gardener's bread and butter material. They come in a bewildering array of leaf patterns – yellow-variegated, white-variegated, blue, lettuce-green, striped, splashed, ribbed – and they are stunning when used *en masse* as beside the stream at SHEFFIELD PARK. Here they contrast with ferns, the grassy foliage of *Iris sibirica*, the pink and white plumes of astilbes, and the flowering candelabra of *Primula pulverulenta*.

Large-leaved plants are especially good weed suppressors and most thrive in damp conditions. The purple-leaved *Ligularia dentata* 'Desdemona' is beautiful all season but its orange flowerheads must be removed as soon as they fade or you will have seedlings everywhere. Its green cut-leaved cousin, *L. przewalskii*, is lovely at WAKEHURST PLACE, but it is very invasive. *Darmera peltata* (formerly *Peltiphyllum peltatum*), which grows beside the lake at SHEFFIELD PARK, looks much like a small gunnera in the landscape and has interesting flesh-pink flowers in early spring. And rodgersias and yellow and white skunk cabbage (*Lysichiton americanus* and *L. camtschatcensis*) prove their worth in the Stream Garden at HIDCOTE.

In a mild humid climate such as that of TRENGWAINTON on the tip of Cornwall, all sorts of adventurous plantings can be attempted and the stream edges boast tree ferns, Chatham Island forget-me-nots, ginger lilies and leathery evergreen *Blechnum chilense*. But there are many ingredients here which can be grown in other parts of Britain. Day-lilies, *Aruncus dioicus*, *Euphorbia sikkimensis*, kingcups and cimicifugas are all perfectly hardy, and so, if they can be grown in deep mud, are the white and green forms of arum lily, *Zantedeschia aethiopica*.

Exotic plants, naturally planted, turns BODNANT into a fantasy landscape, an idealized version of a Himalayan valley.

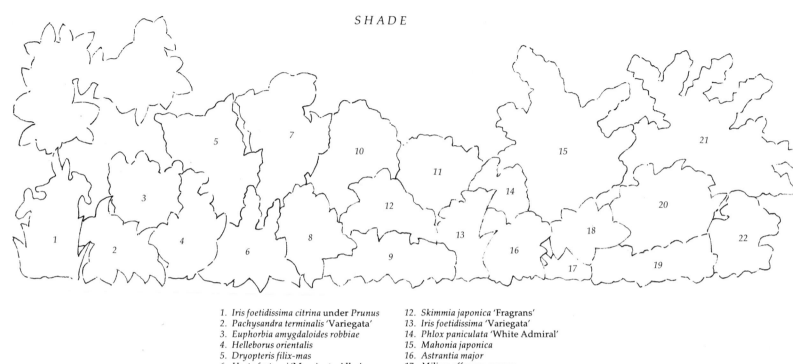

1. *Iris foetidissima citrina* under *Prunus*
2. *Pachysandra terminalis* 'Variegata'
3. *Euphorbia amygdaloides robbiae*
4. *Helleborus orientalis*
5. *Dryopteris filix-mas*
6. *Hosta fortunei* 'Marginata Alba'
7. *Aruncus dioicus*
8. *Anemone × hybrida*
9. *Geranium macrorrhizum album*
10. *Skimmia japonica* 'Veitchii'
11. *Skimmia japonica* 'Veitchii'

12. *Skimmia japonica* 'Fragrans'
13. *Iris foetidissima* 'Variegata'
14. *Phlox paniculata* 'White Admiral'
15. *Mahonia japonica*
16. *Astrantia major*
17. *Milium effusum aureum*
18. *Pulmonaria saccharata*
19. *Geranium macrorrhizum album*
20. *Hemerocallis lilio-asphodelus* (syn. *H. flava*)
21. *Rhamnus alaternus* 'Argenteovariegata'
22. *Anemone × hybrida*

SUN

1. *Potentilla* 'Katherine Dykes'
2. *Viburnum × burkwoodii* 'Park Farm'
3. *Iris pallida* 'Variegata'
4. *Geranium* 'Johnson's Blue'
5. *Rosa rugosa* 'Alba'
6. *Ruta graveolens* 'Jackman's Blue'
7. *Salvia officinalis* 'Purpurascens'
8. *Euphorbia characias*
9. *Hemerocallis lilio-asphodelus* (syn. *H. flava*)
10. *Acanthus spinosus*
11. *Viola cornuta* (Violet)

12. *Bergenia purpurascens*
13. *Geranium* 'Johnson's Blue'
14. *Senecio* 'Sunshine'
15. *Stachys byzantina* (syn. *S. lanata*)
16. *Hebe albicans*
17. *Cytisus × praecox*
18. *Polygonum affine* 'Superbum'
19. *Euphorbia polychroma*
20. *Berberis thunbergii atropurpurea*
21. *Helleborus argutifolius* (syn. *H. corsicus*)
22. *Ruscus aculeatus*

PRACTICAL MATTERS

Ground-cover planting may sound like the answer to every ham-fisted gardener's prayers but some cultural knowledge and attention is still required. Firstly, the soil has to be properly cleaned and prepared ready for planting. Young ground-cover plants cannot be expected to battle with established weeds or to thrive in soil devoid of nutrients, so the same initial care must be directed at areas intended for labour-saving planting as for other areas.

All unwanted trees and shrubs must be cut down and dug out, either by hand or by machine. If there are perennial weeds present – ground-elder, bindweed, nettles, creeping buttercup, etc. – you should spray the remaining vegetation with a weedkiller before rotovating or digging. (These activities simply turn over the soil and chop up the roots; the next season the weeds just pop up again reinvigorated.) Glyphosate is a good systemic weedkiller; it is absorbed by the plants and slowly suffocates them, but leaves no residue in the soil. Apply it when growth is lush and give a second application a month later and a third further on in the year. If you are a committed organic gardener you could stretch heavy black polythene over the ground and leave it in place, anchored by bricks or rocks, for a complete growing season. Horsetail, bindweed and ground elder will take two seasons to vanish if covered with polythene.

It is important to eliminate perennial weeds before undertaking any sort of planting, but especially important before introducing ground-cover subjects. Trying to extract weeds from a dense knotted carpet of plants is a hopeless task. Indeed, there is a warning here. It is that labour-saving planting can very quickly become labour-intensive planting if weeds are allowed to get a hold. I have come across numerous examples of this metamorphosis in private and even National Trust gardens and numerous gardeners cursing themselves for planting too soon or not tackling a subsequent weed infiltration early enough. For even after your ground-cover plants are established a beady eye must be trained on them.

Once you are happy that the ground is clear of perennial weeds (annual weeds you can ignore) – and this will probably be some months later, in the autumn – you can rotovate or hand dig. Go down a spade's depth if possible and remove any large pieces of debris. Now is the time to incorporate some humus (compost, ground bark, leaf-mould or well-rotted manure) to improve the soil's texture and fertility, and to scatter some slow-release organic fertilizer. The ground is now ready for planting, though cautious gardeners may wish to wait a further period to spray weeds again and delay planting until next spring.

The first plants to introduce are the trees and shrubs. Bare-rooted plants (i.e. those lifted straight from the nursery growing fields – a good and cheaper way of acquiring the larger subjects) are usually installed in November, except for evergreens which should go in during September (or, even better, April) as they are more vulnerable in winter and need some growing time beforehand. Containerized plants (the majority of plants are acquired in plastic pots and liners) are best installed in September or in March/April but can be planted throughout the growing season; April is the best month for introducing containerized evergreens.

Dig generous planting holes, loosening the soil all around and working in some more humus and fertilizer. Water well after planting. It is hard to generalize about planting distances but even though the idea is to produce dense labour-saving schemes, I would avoid the temptation to plant subjects shoulder to shoulder, as in a very few years the planting will look congested and the ingredients will suffer from the competition. The goal is, after all, an attractive garden composition, not a coarse thicket.

In any case, herbaceous perennials can happily occupy the middle ground between shrubs for an interim period. Spring and autumn are the traditional seasons for lifting, splitting and planting such plants, but containerized subjects can be installed at any time providing the ground is not waterlogged, frozen or baked. If the soil has been well prepared, you can just make a good hole with a trowel or spade and pop

Some plants can be pulled apart by hand, such as this *Iris foetidissima*. A number of small portions usually give a faster covering.

A layer of mulch between plants helps to retain moisture and keep weeds at bay.

your plants in; if not, work in some compost and a little fertilizer first. Water well. The ground-cover perennials will make a carpet quicker if you put in lots of small pieces of plant material rather than a few big clumps, so use a knife or a couple of garden forks, back to back, to produce a quantity of rooted portions. Even a newly purchased container plant may be a candidate for immediate subdivision. Avoid planting too closely to the young trees and shrubs which will benefit from several years free of surface competition.

Bulbs go in last or they will be in danger of accidental mutilation. Spring and early summer flowering bulbs are usually planted in September/October; late summer and autumn flowering bulbs in April, except for colchicums which are planted in August. But if you are acquiring bulbs from friends' gardens or dividing them in your own garden, you can lift and transplant as soon as flowering is over, while the plants are still 'in the green' (showing green leaves); snowdrops, cyclamen and winter aconites certainly prefer being moved at this time. Some bulbs like to grow very shallowly, their noses protruding or sitting just below the surface of the soil – cardiocrinums, Madonna lilies and nerines, for example – but the majority should probably be at a depth equivalent to at least twice their width (measure at the widest point). I am indebted to Ursula Buchan for this handy rule of thumb.

Aftercare of ground-cover schemes is simply a matter of being observant and taking action as soon as problems are identified. Until your plants are established you may need to carry out some hoeing or hand-weeding. A mulch of compost or pulverized bark (or grit on beds intended for sun-loving shrubs like rosemary, cistus, phlomis and hebe), spread 50-75mm / 2-3in thick, will spare you even this chore. Occasionally you may need to carry out some pruning to remove dead wood or restore a shrub's shape: take the centre out of a colony of perennials which has become bare and feeble over the years, fill the gap with fresh soil and replant; or apply organic fertilizer to encourage better growth and flowering. But your only real worry is perennial weeds; as soon as you see any, dig them out or spray with a selective weedkiller immediately.

NATURAL PLANTING AND WILDFLOWER MEADOWS

The supreme stage of informal and labour-saving gardening is where the demarcation lines between borders and lawns collapse entirely. Instead of being confined to prescribed compartments, groups of trees and shrubs are positioned 'casually' around the site to suggest a woodland or open country setting; climbing plants ramble through them or flop over banks, rocks or fallen branches; and herbaceous perennials and bulbs grow and seed themselves wherever they can become established – on the fringes of plantations, in walls, between rocks and in the grass.

This type of 'natural' gardening is appealing to many, certainly to me, for it is really an idealization of the countryside which is so rapidly vanishing all around us, a chance to create a refuge for wildflowers, for wildlife and, of course, for oneself. But although it looks as if successful 'natural' gardens spring entirely from a mixture of *ad hoc* planting and benign neglect, they require as much planning as any other sort of garden. Unless you are careful, they can quickly disintegrate into ugly wastelands of impenetrable undergrowth and decay. Chaos will only be avoided if you have an overall vision of what effects you are trying to create, choose the right plants and introduce them into the right places, organize a sympathetic but definite maintenance routine, and keep access paths and arenas of short grass to counter the sense of untidiness and congestion which may sometimes arise.

Pools of different ground-cover plants enliven the nuttery at SISSINGHURST CASTLE, *Kent. Geranium and white trillium contrast with the lime-green flowerheads of euphorbia and smyrnium, with* Rhododendron luteum *behind.*

Most people will prefer the garden to be neat around the house and to become progressively more casual as you move towards the boundaries. But it should be realized that very dramatic effects can be achieved by having an abrupt transition near the house. At MONTACUTE, only the stone walls of the courts separate cows and buttercups from lawns and topiary and at CASTLE DROGO the wild moor, with its gorse and bracken, sweeps right up to the battlements on several sides.

WOODLAND HABITATS

When gardening in a woodland style, the principle of contraction and expansion within the design is worth following closely. You do not want to end up with a site that is solid with foliage and uniformly overcast. You want paths that periodically open out completely into clearings and glades; thickets of shrubs that make way occasionally for specimen trees; a tapestry of sunlight and shadow.

Planting can be carried out in layers, as described in the ground-cover chapter. Evergreen trees, and deciduous trees with dense foliage or very large leaves, such as chestnut, beech and sycamore, are best used in or on the edge of clearings, or as boundary subjects, for their canopy will be too heavy for most plants to grow underneath. Lighter deciduous trees like oak, ash, amelanchier and larch permit interesting lower layers, consisting of mixed evergreen and deciduous shrubs, shade-tolerant perennials and varieties of bulbs.

Plant groups may be arranged as in very informal ground-cover planting, the ingredients being allowed to interweave fairly freely. But the lower layer may be allowed

Bluebells at BODNANT, *Gwynedd.*

Bluebells, campions and ferns grow between rhododendrons on the grassy banks at LANHYDROCK, *Cornwall, as they do in many of the Trust's woodland gardens. Note the dramatic sweep of the entrance drive.*

to spill out into the adjacent rough lawn. Some grow equally well in soil as in thin grass, and permitting them to do so helps to suggest that this really is a natural idyll rather than a man-made garden. Good candidates for such fringe planting are ferns, bluebells, foxgloves, geraniums, deadnettles (*Lamium* species), primroses, anemones, red campion (*Silene dioica*) and Solomon's seal.

At LANHYDROCK the steep banks of the Woodland Garden are smothered in snowdrops, pheasant's eye narcissus and bluebells, and there are many naturalized primroses, foxgloves, red campions and ferns. To keep the banks tidy and to prevent coarser weeds from getting a hold, the spring bulb foliage is raked away once it has withered and the wildflowers are scythed after they have flowered and dispersed their seed. The ferns are left untouched, as they are on the bluebell banks at COTEHELE and GLENDURGAN, where a strimmer is used to level the rank growth around them in mid-June. Where there is grass, further monthly cuts are necessary.

Autumn- and winter-flowering cyclamen thrive in dry soil under trees.

Where the soil is dry, there is no better plant for naturalizing than cyclamen. Autumn-flowering *C. hederifolium* thrives under a great blue cedar at KILLERTON, under pines and sweet chestnuts at KNIGHTSHAYES and under larches at GREYS COURT; and at SALTRAM there are carpets of both pink and white forms in the Lime Avenue. Winter-flowering *C. coum* is also in evidence at GREYS COURT, in the dry dark shade of a yew; just before the seed is about to drop, the plants are lightly strimmed and the seed scattered, and thanks to this treatment, a good colony has been established.

You do not need a wood to make a woodland garden. A single tree or stand of shrubs is enough to provide the dappled shade necessary for woodland perennials and bulbs. Circles of rough grass are left around trees in the lawns at SALTRAM, creating miniature habitats for bluebells, and at COTEHELE cyclamen have been planted in the lawn around the boles of a tulip tree and a yellow ash. Such Lilliputian compositions are always endearing.

Apart from growing plants under and around trees and shrubs, you can also grow plants up them. Ivy and old man's beard *(Clematis flammula)* wander freely at SNOWSHILL, as do honeysuckles at STANDEN. At CLEVEDON COURT pink *Clematis*

Honeysuckle (Lonicera)

montana rubens scrambles up yew, and at COTEHELE up cherry laurel. Climbing roses are trained up the fruit trees in the orchard at SISSINGHURST, and at KNIGHTSHAYES rambling roses grow up pines. But these last – which include white multifloras, *R. filipes* and pink 'Paul's Himalayan Musk' – are brought to the ground every three to five years to be pruned. This is not a job an amateur gardener would relish! In a wilder setting, and given very large host trees, this would not be necessary.

Of all the plants that trees can support, mistletoe is the one that most suggests a mature natural community. It thrives on the cider apple trees in the orchard at BARRINGTON COURT, but will also grow well on hawthorns and mountain ash. To establish it, it is usually enough to press the ripe berries into cracks on the undersides of young branches in March. Being evergreen, the balls of growth, like green rook's nests, are especially valuable in the winter garden.

Mistletoe (Viscum album)

Open Habitats

Groups of shrubs grown in open positions also make informal labour-saving features. Whether they are surrounded by grass or banked against the garden's boundary, they can be left to develop freely and knit together casually. For an apparently natural composition, highly ornamental shrubs should be avoided. Instead of flamboyant flowers and coloured leaves, you want greenery, simple blossom and berries; the garden at SNOWSHILL is an inspiration. Some of the best candidates are native shrubs like hazel, holly, spindle *(Euonymus europaeus)* and guelder rose *(Viburnum opulus)* supplemented by small trees like bird cherry *(Prunus padus)*, hawthorn and field maple *(Acer campestre)*. But foreigners such as amelanchier, white-berried symphoricarpos, laurel, philadelphus and cotoneaster are also excellent. Great favourites of mine for neo-native plantings are the dwarf chestnuts, especially *Aesculus parviflora*. This 3m / 10ft shrub is grown at SHUGBOROUGH and is usefully late-flowering – scented white bottlebrushes in August. It is a mystery why it and its relatives are so seldom seen.

Viburnum opulus

The native cuckoo pint, Arum maculatum,
*produces its curious flowers in spring. They are followed
by drumsticks of orange berries.*

A hedge of natives, trimmed in summer (but not as ferociously as farmers insist) is also pleasing and helps to soften the contrast between garden and countryside. Haw-thorn is the best material and should perhaps be the dominant ingredient but field maple, privet, holly, guelder rose, dogwood and dog rose are fine complementary candi-dates. The more mixed the hedging the better.

More contrived, but still varied enough not to appear formal, is a tapestry hedge. Here traditional hedging plants like yew, box, beech, holly and hornbeam are interwoven. There are famous examples in the Fuchsia Garden at HIDCOTE. These do contain copper beech and variegated hollies, but touches of leaf colour are hardly noticeable at a distance if they are dominated by quantities of green, and I am sure you

could include such plants in a boundary hedge, too, without disrupting the harmonious transition to the countryside beyond.

Shrubberies and hedgerows can be underplanted with all the plants which enjoy a woodland-fringe habitat. In addition to the plants mentioned above, you could try lords and ladies *(Arum maculatum)*, with their arrowhead leaves in winter and drumsticks of orange berries in summer, helle-bores, lily-of-the-valley, and that indispensable evergreen iris, *I. foetidissima.*

On retentive ground, willows and dogwoods can form the mainstay of a shrubbery. Few gardeners seem to think of willows in a shrubby context: their minds are on monstrous weeping trees, I suppose. But there are many 3m / 10ft varieties which are highly desirable; some have striking winter stems – brilliantly coloured in *Salix alba* forms; some have wonderful catkins (notably *S. gracilistyla* and the black-catkined *S. g.* 'Melanostachys'), and some have good silvery leaves (*S. alba sericea* is the best). All are natural enough for the wild garden, as are the equally neglected and moisture-loving clethras (pink or white plumes in late summer) and aronias (fiery autumn foliage and berries).

In the company of the odd moisture-loving tree like alder and taxodium, they will also make fine pond or streamside inhabitants. But water really needs to be open to the sky as much as possible, and its banks left largely uncluttered. You want to be able to wander around the grass edge and to enjoy the reflections of sun and clouds. So use shrubs sparingly and confine them to specific areas. The same applies to clumps of pondside perennials. Small groups on the pond's corners or a sweep down just one or two sides is preferable to an unbroken ring of growth which denies access.

Areas of near-natural woodland at BODNANT *give respite
from the multicoloured displays of rhododendrons. Green
leaves and reflections on water make the most tranquil scenes,
and by midsummer, much of the valley is as calm as this.*

At ERDDIG a single stand of *Polygonum campanulatum* (now *Persicaria campanulata*) – a lovely summer-flowering plant with fluffy pale pink heads – is enough to give some vertical interest to the empty canal edge. This is just the sort of unselfconscious perennial that suits the 'natural' garden. Unlike gaudy day-lilies and painted hostas, it could be mistaken for a wispy native; in fact it comes from the Himalayas. Another good candidate is the meadow-sweet *(Filipendula ulmaria),* which has scented cream plumes in early summer. It grows beside the lake at STOURHEAD with rushes and nettles.

On those parts of the water's edge bare of plants, the grass can be left slightly tall. You are not going to be able to mow right to the edge anyway, so you may as well designate a thin strip as 'rough' rather than worry about it every time you are cutting the lawn. You can strim it a few times a year.

MEADOW GARDENING

Connecting and unifying all the garden's features and plant groups is the grass carpet. In the traditional ordered garden, grass provides the foil for and the respite from the dramas played out by the other areas of vegetation. But in the natural garden the grass itself can entertain. It can flaunt flowers and wave seedheads and turn itself into one of the main sources of colour and seasonal interest.

Having flowering plants growing in the grass is, as I mentioned previously, the obvious next step in 'alternative' lawn management. In fact, as soon as weedkillers are discontinued, you will notice the gradual appearance of colonizing wildflowers. The mowing routine that you practise will determine which plants these are. In the close-cropped lawn, they will be the low-growing flora which you formerly despised as lawn weeds – daisies, blue speedwell, clover, plantains and yellow cat's ear. Now you can enjoy them with a clear conscience instead of struggling to preserve an immaculate sward. Any ingredients that you do not want – dandelions, perhaps – can be eliminated with a spot weedkiller. And any plants that you want to introduce –

such as creeping thyme or creeping mint – can be inserted; use young plants with a good potful of roots and remove a small plug of turf to accommodate them.

Normal weekly mowing, cutting to a height of 18mm/¾in, will promote the spread of these plants, but at peak flowering time, in late May and early June, you can then take a short break. At ANTONY HOUSE mowing of part of the lawn stops in August, to allow ladies' tresses orchids to appear, and resumes after the flowering is over (they do not seem to set seed so there is no need to wait for dispersal). At UPPARK the orchids do set seed, but the seedheads have to be protected from pheasants! If you grow small spring bulbs in the lawn, such as snowdrops, aconites and crocuses, the pause will be at the start of the season; mowing will begin six weeks after the last performer has finished.

The chequered flowers of snakeshead fritillaries appear in the damp grass at BATEMAN'S, Sussex.

*An assortment of wildflowers grow in
Nellson's Piece at* COTEHELE, *Cornwall. Mowing is delayed
at least until the end of June.*

An important point to stress is that for flowering plants to thrive, the grass must be relatively weak and the soil poor. Few subjects can compete with a thick, lush sward. On no account, therefore, should fertilizers be used either on wildflower lawns or meadow areas; grass clippings should also be removed. If you are starting with a conventional fertile lawn and converting to 'alternative' methods, it may take several years of starvation to weaken the sward sufficiently for flower colonization. Alternatively, you might consider taking up the turf (or poisoning and rotovating) and re-sowing using a finer grass/wildflower mix.

Where the grass is higher and subject to less frequent cuts, few of the low lawn 'weeds' can survive. The flora that will appear here will be taller and wispier; but the season of performance depends on your mowing routine. To encourage spring flowers to colonize, the grass must not be mown at all at least until the end of June. By this time the early performers will have had the chance to flower and set seed. But afterwards regular mowing, cutting to a height of 75-100mm / 3-4in is necessary to prevent the grass and coarser weeds from becoming dominant. At COTEHELE, which has a one-acre wildflower garden, this routine suits lady's smocks/milkmaids/cuckoo flower *(Cardamine pratensis),* bluebells, cowslips and orchids, as well as a host of daffodils. Blue bugle and purple self-heal *(Prunella vulgaris)* also do well under this routine and, if your ground is damp, you can also expect snakeshead fritillaries to succeed. These delightful plants, with large pendent chequered cups, stain my local water meadow (at Magdalen College, Oxford) with reddish-purple every May.

For summer flowers a different routine has to be adopted: the grass can be mown in the spring but it must be left uncut through the summer months.

At SHEFFIELD PARK the meadow is essentially summer-flowering and often receives an early trim; thereafter it is left to become a mass of flowers (including thousands of spotted orchids) and is not cut again until the very end of August.

Many National Trust meadows combine spring and summer flowers in the same area. At SIZERGH CASTLE the meadow garden is not cut at all until late August or early September. By then there have been a succession of flowers. In spring there are wild daffodils *(Narcissus pseudonarcissus)*, sweet violets, early orchids (purple *Orchis mascula* and green-winged *O. morio*) and double-flowered lady's smocks; in summer, ox-eye daisies, *(Leucanthemum vulgare)* cranesbills, bugle, bird's foot trefoil *(Lotus corniculatus)* fox and cubs *(Hieracium aurantiacum)*, twayblade *(Listera ovata)* and greater butterfly orchids *(Platanthera chlorantha)*, and a range of flowering grasses; and the season concludes with betony, hardheads *(Centaurea nigra)* and red-fruited *Arum maculatum*.

By August such mixed meadow areas may be becoming too untidy for comfort, so a cut early in the month can be contemplated. This may mean missing out on a few late-summer species, but that cannot be helped. A second cut at the end of August will leave the ground an ideal length for the autumn performers – pink, purple and white colchicums and autumn crocuses. If you have distinct spring and summer meadow areas, the former is the best place for these latecomers. Regular cutting from the end of June onwards will have produced a neat green haze, against which the bulbs show up well. Cease mowing in late August to allow the flowers to emerge. All meadow areas should receive a final cut in mid-November.

In very large gardens, a flail mower is an attractive investment for cutting meadow grass. This has a series of free-moving blades, mounted on a rotary cylinder. Brush cutters are also useful for grass fringes – around trees, shrubs and fences. They have a high-speed rotating disc to which nylon cord flails are attached; the front-mounted wheeled model, petrol-driven, is probably the best, being quieter and

The famous wildflower bank at SIZERGH,
Cumbria, is not cut at all until the end of the summer. Ox-eye daisies and bright orange fox and cubs, Hieracium aurantiacum, *are among the cast.*

less tiring. There are now powerful mowers, which will tackle meadow cutting quite satisfactorily. Strimmers are efficient at the job and, for the energetic, there is always the scythe. It has to be said that even for National Trust gardeners, cutting on wildflower meadow is not a task greatly enjoyed. It can be hot, hard, dusty work.

There is an enormous range of plants that can be grown in grass. As I have indicated, many species will arrive by themselves and many more can be introduced by the gardener. Certain wildflowers are more successful on certain types of soil. On acid soil, red campion (*Silene dioica*), cornflower (*Centaurea cyanus*), foxglove, white clover and corn marigold (*Chrysanthemum segetum*) thrive. On neutral soil, meadow buttercup (*Ranunculus acris*), common flax

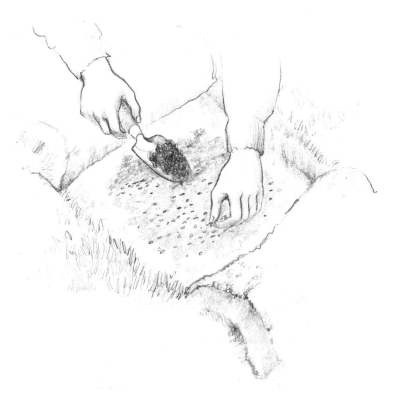

Sewing seed of interesting meadow grasses under a plug of turf.

(*Linum usitatissimum*), yellow rattle (*Rhinanthus minor*) and ragged robin (*Lychnis flos-cuculi*) excel. And on limy and chalky soil, the greatest number of wildflowers prosper, including lady's bedstraw (*Galium verum*), common and greater knapweeds (*Centaurea nigra* and *C. scabiosa*), small scabious (*Scabiosa columbaria*), wild basil (*Clinopodium vulgare*) and wild carrot (*Daucus carota*).

But it is always worth trying interesting species, for many seem to grow well whatever the pH. Ox-eye daisies (*Leucanthemum vulgare*), bluebells, harebells (*Campanula rotundifolia*), cowslips, self-heal (*Prunella vulgaris*), black medick (*Medicago lupulina*) and bird's foot trefoil are examples.

Native grasses and clovers are easily introduced by seed. Remove a small plug of grass in the autumn or spring, loosen the soil underneath and put a layer of seed compost on top; then sprinkle in your chosen seeds and water with a fine-hosed can. Other native perennials are best introduced as small plants. These can be bought from a specialist nursery or they can be grown from seed, potted up and transferred to the meadow the following autumn. Fresh seed seems to be important for good germination of natives – cowslips and geraniums, for example. Orchids are notoriously difficult to raise from seed, because they need companion fungi as a nutrient source when young. A further method of introducing broadleaved natives is to insert whole turves which already contain plants; this is being done at ANTONY HOUSE to establish primroses in new areas.

So far I have presumed you already have a lawn. If you do not, then you can sow one which has wildflowers in the mix at the outset. Several firms market wildflower/grass seed. Preparation of the ground is the same as for conventional lawns except that no fertilizers are added. Autumn is the best time for sowing. In the early years it is sensible to give the grass a cut at the beginning of the season, in April, to prevent it from suffocating the other flora.

As wildflower gardeners we are playing a valuable part in helping to preserve the country's heritage. Half of Britain's flower-rich meadows have been destroyed or severely

Ground-cover plants are so thoroughly interwoven at STANDEN *that the borders seem to be entirely the work of nature. Here white-edged hosta makes a backdrop for the flowers of bugle, tellima and* Geranium nodosum.

damaged in the last fifteen years. Many of our wetlands and ancient woodlands have also been lost. Anything that we do as gardeners to create natural habitats and keep populations of native plants going is a contribution to the cause of conservation. But of course our efforts become meaningless if in order to make our little reserve, we have ripped the heart out of another one. So we must be disciplined about never helping ourselves to plants growing in the wild; there are now plenty of specialist growers and seedsmen who can cater more than adequately for our needs.

WILDFLOWERS I

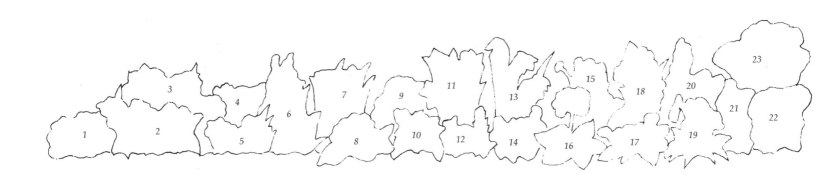

1. *Cyclamen coum*
2. *Galanthus nivalis*
3. *Eranthis hyemalis*
4. *Crocus tommasinianus*
5. *Crocus flavus* (syn. *C. aureus*)
6. *Narcissus cyclamineus*
7. *Narcissus pseudonarcissus*
8. *Primula vulgaris*
9. *Anemone apennina*
10. *Anemone nemorosa*
11. *Large daffodils*
12. *Ajuga reptans*

13. *Fritillaria meleagris*
14. *Ranunculus ficaria*
15. *Cardamine pratensis*
16. *Primula veris*
17. *Taraxacum officinale*
18. *Narcissus poeticus*
19. Bluebells (*Hyacinthoides non-scripta*)
20. *Orchis mascula*
21. *Sanguisorba minor*
22. *Orchis morio*
23. *Anthriscus sylvestris*

WILDFLOWERS II

1. Lilium martagon
2. Geranium pratense
3. Hypochoeris radicata
4. Vicia cracca
5. Prunella vulgaris
6. Hieracium aurantiacum
7. Rumex acetosella
8. Listera ovata
9. Lotus corniculatus
10. Filipendula ulmaria
11. Achillea millefolium
12. Malva moschata

13. Leontodon hispidus
14. Leucanthemum vulgare
15. Stachys officinalis
16. Centaurea scabiosa
17. Galium verum
18. Knautia arvensis
19. Crocus speciosus
20. Colchicum autumnale
21. Crocus nudiflorus
22. Crocus kotschyanus
23. Cyclamen hederifolium
24. Colchicum speciosum

If you are a purist, you will confine yourself to British plants in your wildflower meadow. But there is a host of foreign or garden-derived ingredients which can share their home. Daffodils are obvious candidates. Of course, we do have native narcissi, the Lent lily (*N. pseudonarcissus*), and the Tenby daffodil (*N. p. obvallaris*), which are ideal in grass, but there are many other outstanding varieties; twenty-seven forms are grown in grass at COTEHELE. The old Barrii narcissi are a great feature in many National Trust gardens, including Cothele – very graceful and not so blowsy that they look out of place when naturalized. All the big strong hybrids look well in grass, as long as they are planted in separate drifts; groups of mixed colours and shapes present a muddled and unsympathetic picture. In fact, tall daffodils are better here than in the border; green is a more effective foil for the flowers than brown, and the rising grass drowns their dying foliage. WIMPOLE HALL has a fine collection, including bright yellows like 'King Alfred', 'Golden Harvest' and 'Carlton' and the creamy-white 'Mount Hood'.

Many people prefer to see the simpler and smaller-flowered daffodils in their meadow. These at least look as if they might be natives. The season can begin in March with the tiny hoop petticoat (*N. bulbocodium*), particularly in its lemon variety *citrinus*; continue through April with short *N. cyclamineus* and its hybrids ('February Gold', 'February Silver', white 'Jenny', yellow 'Peeping Tom'); and conclude in May with the tall scented pheasant's eye sorts, *N. poeticus* and 'Actaea'.

If you are growing only daffodils in your grass, you should leave the grass uncut until at least six weeks after the last bulbs have flowered. This will be in mid-June. But the dead heads can be strimmed away as soon as the flowers are over, to prevent the bulbs wasting energy by producing seed; you may, however, want the species narcissi to seed themselves, of course.

Daffodils look good in grass and their dying leaves are less obtrusive here than in borders. They are as at home under an apple tree in a small garden as in great drifts at STOURHEAD.

There are so many bulbs suitable for naturalizing that you can maintain colour right through the spring. Single- and double-flowered snowdrops, golden winter aconites (*Eranthis hyemalis*), orange *Crocus flavus (C. aureus)*, and violet and mauve *C. tommasinianus* supply colour from late February through March; chunky *Crocus vernus* varieties can be added too, if you do not think them too artificial – they look well at LACOCK ABBEY. In late March through April there are the daffodils, together with white, lavender and blue anemones (*A. nemorosa, A. blanda* and *A. apennina*). And in late April through May there are English and Spanish bluebells, spiky blue camassias (*C. esculenta*), the pheasant's eye narcissus and some tulips. Red Darwin tulips thrive at SISSINGHURST, but the large hybrids do not usually persist (with the exception of the tenacious Darwin hybrids). Our native *Tulipa sylvestris*, a slender yellow, is more reliable and can be seen in grass at ACORN BANK; wispy *T. turkestanica* and *T. tarda* are also worth trying, as is scarlet *T. sprengeri*. If the ground is dampish, the spring (February) and summer (April) snowflakes (*Leucojum vernum* and *L. aestivum*), are delightful ingredients; *L. aestivum* is a British native. Both have white, green-tipped bells. June-flowering martagon lilies, as seen at MONTACUTE, grow well in thin grass.

For an autumn flush, *Crocus speciosus*, which comes in many shades of lavender and violet-blue, rosy *C. kotschyanus* and purple *C. nudiflorus* are the most reliable. They will soon seed and swell into rivers of colour which flow into nearby flowerbeds as well as over short grass. Colchicums give altogether more substantial flowers, great glistening chalices of pink, rose, lilac, mauve and white. *Colchicum autumnale* and, even better, *C. speciosum*, are the species to plunder. There is a lovely display of them at POWIS CASTLE, where they are grouped on the grass bank below the terraced borders, beneath fiery-leaved Japanese maples. Colchicum flowers appear naked, so you can mow over them as soon as they have withered away. The leaves, which are lush, broad and straplike, sprout in spring, and you must mow around them until they begin to turn yellow.

In addition to this host of glamorous bulbs, border perennials can also join the throng. Tough, vigorous cranesbills like pink *Geranium × oxonianum* should perform as satisfactorily as the native blue *Geranium pratense*. Oriental poppies are flamboyant ingredients, quite tough enough for grass. They now come in whites, reds, salmons and pinks as well as the conventional orange, and make an unexpected contrast to cow parsley/Queen Anne's lace. Red-hot pokers (*Kniphofia* species) are succeeding in the grass at POWIS CASTLE, and in numerous old private gardens you see peonies competing well. Pastel blue campanulas, like *C. lactiflora* and *C. latifolia* will extend the season into July, as will foxgloves and cream, scented meadowsweet.

WILDLIFE

A happy result of gardening in a relaxed fashion, cultivating wildflowers, encouraging carpeting ground cover, and allowing areas of grass to grow long, is that more birds, mammals and insects take up residence. The wildlife in National Trust gardens is rich and varied. You can see grebe on the lake at STOURHEAD, red squirrels at WALLINGTON, slow-worms at KILLERTON. woodcock at ACORN BANK, and a host of rare butterflies at SHEFFIELD PARK and WAKEHURST PLACE. At GREYS

Black-necked grebes.

COURT alone there are dormice nesting in the wisteria pergola, hedgehogs hibernating in clumps of lithospermum, great crested newts in the lily pond, and kestrels in the tower! The cow pond here, which is only 9 × 23.5m / 30 × 80ft, has now become a miniature wildlife sanctuary. Three tench were installed to keep the water sweet; and willo-wherb, rushes, teasel and brambles were allowed to establish themselves around the willows. Now toads, newts, ducks and grass-snakes live in and around the pond. Goldcrests flit among the branches, green woodpeckers visit, and English partridge nest near by. Habitats for wildlife are being deliberately created in many Trust gardens, and at WALLING-TON shrubby lonicera is planted in front of yew to prevent deer from grazing on the poisonous leaves – deer dislike lonicera.

Of course, animals are not always the gardener's best friends. Fallow deer and muntjak jump over the ha-ha at GREYS COURT and strip tree bark. Badgers eat the tulips at STANDEN (they smell them out even under catmint!); and at GLENDURGAN badgers are tunnelling in the cherry laurel maze – which is quite a hazard for the public. Moles are a problem in many gardens; trapping is the best way of getting rid of them, although old tricks such as putting holly and caper spurge in their runs sometimes work. One of the worst animal offenders is the peacock, an aristocratic inhabitant of many of the grander Trust gardens. Apart from the fact that they enjoy scratching the ground, they delight in crash-landing on top of pots freshly planted with delicate annuals. But the added interest of watching animals is always worth the trouble they may cause – well, nearly always.

A weed or a food source for wildlife? Your attitude to dandelions changes when you see Peacock butterflies alighting.

SHADE-TOLERANT PLANTS

Shrubs

Acer palmatum Japanese maple
Arundinaria bamboo
Berberis (except purple forms)
Camellia
Chaenomeles ornamental quince or japonica
Cotoneaster
Elaeagnus
Enkianthus
Escallonia
Forsythia
Gaultheria wintergreen
Hydrangea
Hypericum St. John's wort
Ilex holly
Leycesteria formosa Himalayan honeysuckle
Mahonia
Osmanthus
Pieris
Rhododendron
Symphoricarpos snowberry
Viburnum
Vinca periwinkle

Perennials

Ajuga bugle
Alchemilla mollis lady's mantle
Anemone × *hybrida* Japanese anemone
Aruncus dioicus goat's beard
Astrantia masterwort
Bergenia
Brunnera
Convallaria
Cyclamen
Doronicum
Ferns
Geranium cranesbill
Helleborus hellebore
Hemerocallis daylily
Hosta
Iris Pacific Coast hybrids
Omphalodes
Phlox alpine
Polygonum (now *Persicaria*) knotweed
Pulmonaria lungwort
Saxifraga × *urbium* London pride
Speirantha convallarioides
Symphytum comfrey
Tellima grandiflora rubra
Tiarella
Trachystemon orientalis
Viola labradorica purpurea

PLANTS FOR DEEP SHADE, DRY SOIL

Shrubs

Aucuba
Buxus box

Euonymus evergreen varieties
× *Fatshedera*
Fatsia
Hedera helix ivy
Hypericum calycinum rose of Sharon
Lonicera nitida, L. pileata shrubby honeysuckle
Pachysandra terminalis
Prunus laurocerasus Cherry laurel
Prunus lusitanica Portugal laurel
Rubus tricolor
Sarcococca Christmas box
Skimmia
Taxus yew
Vinca periwinkle

Perennials

Alchemilla conjuncta
Asarum
Blechnum ferns
Dryopteris filix-mas male fern
Epimedium
Euphorbia amygdaloides robbiae Mrs Robb's bonnet
Hemerocallis fulva daylily
Iris foetidissima Gladwin iris
Lamium deadnettle
Symphytum grandiflorum comfrey
Trachystemon orientalis
Vancouveria
Waldsteinia ternata

SUN-LOVING SHRUBS

Shrubs

Erica heather
Fuchsia
Hamamelis witch hazel
Hebe

Lonicera syringantha
Philadelphus
Photinia
Potentilla
Rosa rose
Senecio 'Sunshine' (now *Brachyglottis* 'Sunshine')
Stephanandra
Viburnum

Perennials

Bergenia
Campanula portenschlagiana
Geranium cranesbill
Heuchera
Veronica gentianoides
Viola cornuta

PLANTS FOR FULL SUN, DRY SOIL

Shrubs

Artemisia
Ballot pseudodictamnus
Ceanothus 'Cascade'
Ceratostigma shrubby plumbago
Choisya ternata Mexican orange blossom
Cistus
Cytisus broom
Elaeagnus
Genista broom
Helianthemum
Hyssopus hyssop
Juniperus juniper
Lavandula lavender
Lupinus arboreus tree lupin
Phlomis fruticosa Jerusalem sage
Romneya

Rosmarinus rosemary
Ruta graveolens rue
Salvia sage
Santolina cotton lavender
Yucca

Perennials

Acaena
Acanthus
Achillea
Alyssum
Anthemis
Arabis
Armeria
Aubrieta
Calamintha
Campanula alliariifolia
Cerastium
Crambe
Dianthus
Geranium renardii
Iberis
Iris graminea, I. innominata
Liriope
Nepeta catmint
Ophiopogon
Sedum
Stachys lamb's lugs
Teucrium germander
Thymus thyme

MEADOW FLOWERS

Spring Wildflowers

Ajuga reptans bugle
Anthriscus sylvestris cow parsley
Bellis perennis daisy

Cardamine pratensis lady's smock or milkmaid
Orchis mascula early purple orchid,
    O. morio green-winged orchid
Primula veris cowslip, *P. vulgaris* primrose
Rhinanthus minor yellow rattle
Sanguisorba minor salad burnet
Stellaria graminea lesser stitchwort
Taraxacum officinale dandelion

Spring Bulbs

Anemone apennina, A. blanda, A. nemorosa wood anemone
Camassia esculenta
Crocus tommasinianus, C. aureus, C. sieberi, C. vernus
Eranthis hyemalis winter aconite
Fritillaria meleagris
Hyacinthoides hispanica Spanish bluebell
Leucojum aestivum, L. vernum
Narcissus asturiensis, N. bulbocodium, N. cyclamineus,
    N. poeticus, N. pseudonarcissus Lent lily,
    N. triandrus hybrid daffodils
Ornithogalum nutans
Tulipa sylvestris

Summer wildflowers

Achillea millefolium yarrow
Campanula rotundifolia harebell
Centaurea nigra hardhead, *C. scabiosa* knapweed
Filipendula ulmaria meadowsweet
Galium vernum lady's bedstraw
Geranium pratense meadow geranium
Hieracium aurantiacum orange hawkweed or fox and cubs
Hypochoeris radicata cat's ear
Knautia arvensis field scabious
Leontodon hispidus rough hawkbit
Leucanthemum vulgare ox-eye daisy
Listera ovata common twayblade orchid

Lotus corniculatus bird's foot trefoil
Malva moschata musk mallow
Platanthera chlorantha greater butterfly orchid
Prunella vulgaris self-heal
Ranunculus acris meadow buttercup
Rumex acetosella sheep's sorrel
Salvia pratensis meadow clary
Stachys officinalis betony
Vicia cracca tufted vetch

Summer and Autumn Bulbs

Colchicum autumnale, C. speciosum
Crocus kotschyanus, C. nudiflorus, C. speciosus
Lilium martagon

WILDFLOWERS FOR VERY POOR SOIL

Centaurium centaury
Echium vulgare viper's bugloss
Glaucium flavum yellow horned poppy
Papaver rhoeas field poppy
Sedum stonecrop
Vicia vetch

WILDFLOWERS FOR SHADY AREAS AND WOODLAND FRINGE

Arum maculatum lords and ladies
Chelidonium majus greater celandine
Convallaria majalis lily of the valley
Digitalis purpurea foxglove
Galium odoratum sweet woodruff
Geranium phaeum mourning widow, *G. robertianum* herb
   Robert, *G. sylvaticum* wood cranesbill
Ferns

Fragaria vesca wild strawberry
Helleborus foetidus stinking hellebore
Iris foetidissima Gladwin iris
Lamium deadnettle
Polygonatum Solomon's seal
Primula veris cowslip, *P. vulgaris* primrose
Ranunculus ficaria lesser celandine
Silene dioica red campion
Stachys sylvatica hedge woundwort
Viola riviniana common dog violet

BULBS FOR SHADY AREAS AND WOODLAND FRINGE

Allium ursinum ramsons or wild garlic
Anemone blanda, A. nemorosa wood anemone, *A. sylvestris*
Cyclamen
Eranthis hyemalis winter aconite
Erythronium dens-canis dog's tooth violet
Galanthus nivalis snowdrop
Hyacinthoides hispanica Spanish bluebell,
   H. non-scripta bluebell
Narcissus daffodil

SHRUBS AND SMALL TREES FOR NATURAL COPSES

Acer campestre field maple
Aesculus parviflora
Amelanchier lamarckii snowy mespilus
Buxus sempervirens box
Carpinus betulus hornbeam (may be coppiced)
Clematis
Corylus avellana hazel
Cotoneaster
Crataegus monogyna hawthorn; *C. laevigata*
Euonymus europaeus spindle tree, *E. planipes*
Hedera ivy
Ilex aquifolium holly

Ligustrum privet
Lonicera honeysuckle
Malus sylvestris crab apple
Philadelphus mock orange
Prunus laurocerasus cherry laurel, *P. padus* bird cherry
Rosa rose
Sambucus nigra elder
Sorbus aucuparia rowan
Viburnum opulus guelder rose, *V. lantana* wayfaring tree

SHRUBS AND SMALL TREES FOR NATURAL WATERSIDE PLANTING

Amelanchier lamarckii snowy mespilus
Clethra alnifolia sweet pepper bush
Cornus alba dogwood

Cornus stolonifera 'Flaviramea'
Salix willow (may be coppiced)

WILDFLOWERS FOR WATERSIDE PLANTING

Caltha palustris marsh marigold
Eupatorium cannabinum hemp agrimony
Ferns *Onoclea, Osmunda*
Filipendula ulmaria meadowsweet
Iris pseudacorus sweet flag
Leucojum aestivum summer snowflake, *L. vernum* spring snowflake
Lychnis flos-cuculi ragged robin
Ranunculus acris meadow buttercup
Stachys palustris marsh woundwort

INDEX OF NATIONAL TRUST GARDENS

Acorn Bank Garden,
Temple Sowerby, Penrith, Cumbria
(07683) 61281

Antony House,
Torpoint, Cornwall (0752) 812191

Ashdown House,
Lambourn, Newbury, Berkshire (for
opening times call NT regional office
(0494) 28051)

Bateman's,
Burwash, Etchingham, East Sussex
(0435) 882302

Barrington Court,
Ilminster, Somerset (0460) 40601/52242

Bodnant Garden,
Tal-y-Cafn, Colwyn Bay, Clwyd
(0492) 650460

Buscot Park,
Faringdon, Oxfordshire (0367) 20786

Calke Abbey,
Ticknall, Derbyshire (0332) 863822

Castle Drogo,
Drewsteignton, Devon (06473) 3306

Charlecote Park,
Wellesbourne, Warwickshire
(0789) 470277

Claremont Landscape Garden,
Esher, Surrey (for opening times call NT
regional office (0372) 53401)

Clevedon Court,
Clevedon, Avon (0272) 872257

Clumber Park,
Worksop, Nottinghamshire
(0909) 476592

Cotehele,
St Dominick, Saltash, Cornwall
(0579) 50434

Cragside House and Country Park,
Rothbury, Northumberland (0669) 20333

Dunster Castle,
Minehead, Somerset (0643) 821314

Erddig,
Wrexham, Clwyd (0978) 355314

Felbrigg Hall,
Roughton, Norwich, Norfolk
(026 375) 444

Glendurgen Garden,
Mawnan Smith, Falmouth, Cornwall
(0736) 64378

Greys Court,
Rotherfield Greys, Henley-on-Thames,
Oxfordshire (049 17) 529

Hidcote Manor Garden,
Chipping Campden, Gloucestershire
(0386) 438333

Killerton,
Broadclyst, Exeter, Devon (0392) 881345

Knightshayes Court,
Bolham, Tiverton, Devon (0884) 254665

Lacock Abbey,
Chippenham, Wiltshire (024 973) 227

Lanhydrock,
Bodmin, Cornwall (0208) 73320

Lytes Cary Manor,
Charlton Mackrell, Somerton, Somerset
(for opening times call NT regional office
(0747) 840224)

Montacute House,
Montacute, Somerset (0935) 823289

Moseley Old Hall,
Fordhouses, Wolverhampton,
Staffordshire (0902) 782808

Nymans Garden,
Handcross, Haywards Heath, West Sussex
(0444) 400321/400002

Packwood House,
Lapworth, Solihull, Warwickshire
(056 43) 2024

Polesden Lacey,
Dorking, Surrey (for opening hours call NT
regional office (0372) 53401)

Powis Castle,
Welshpool, Powys (0938) 554336

Saltram,
Plympton, Plymouth, Devon
(0752) 336546

Sheffield Park Garden,
Uckfield, East Sussex (0825) 790655

Shugborough,
Milford, Stafford, Staffordshire
(0889) 881388

Sissinghurst Castle Garden,
Cranbrook, Kent (0580) 712850

Sizergh Castle,
Kendal, Cumbria (053 95) 60070

Snowshill Manor,
Broadway, Gloucestershire (0386) 852410

Standen,
East Grinstead, Sussex (0342) 323029

Stourhead,
Stourton, Warminster, Wiltshire
(0747) 840348

Tintinhull House Garden,
Yeovil, Somerset (for opening times call NT
regional office (0747) 840220)

Trelissick Garden,
Truro, Cornwall (0872) 862090

Trengwainton Garden,
Penzance, Cornwall (0736) 63021

Wakehurst Place Garden,
Ardingly, Haywards Heath, West Sussex
(0444) 892701

Wallington,
Cambo, Morpeth, Northumberland
(067 074) 283

Wimpole Hall,
Arrington, Royston, Hertfordshire
(0223) 207257

BIBLIOGRAPHY AND SELECTED READING

Baines, Chris, *How to Make a Wildlife Garden*, Elm Tree Books, 1985

Brookes, John, *The New Small Garden*, Dorling Kindersley, 1989

Buchan, Ursula, *The Pleasures of Gardening*, Dent, 1987

Hobhouse, Penelope, *The National Trust Book of Gardening*, Pavilion, 1986

Lloyd, Christopher, *The Well-Tempered Garden*, Collins, 1970

The Royal Horticultural Society's Encyclopaedia of Practical Gardening, Mitchell Beazley, 1980

INDEX

Numbers in **BOLD** refer to photographs.

ACKNOWLEDGEMENTS

All the National Trust gardeners I visited while researching this book were extremely generous with their time and wisdom and I offer them my sincere thanks. To Tony Lord I owe a specific debt for allowing me to draw on his broad expertise of all things horticultural. And finally my thanks go to Penelope Hobhouse for asking me to contribute to this series, Penny David for editing my text, and the staff at Pavilion for keeping calm as deadlines passed.

The publishers wish to thank the National Trust and its photographers for their kind permission to reproduce the following photographs:

Andrew Besley: p. 41; **John Bethell:** p. 15; **Michael Brown:** pp. 59, 62; **Neil Campbell-Sharp:** pp. 8, 12, 18, 39; **Linda Covington:** p. 82; **Nigel Forster:** pp. 6, 10, 22, 32; **Joan Gravell:** p. 93; **Jerry Harpur:** p. 42/3; **Marianne Majerus:** p. 49; **Nick Meers:** pp. 25, 30, 65; **National Trust Photographic Library:** pp. 33, 35; **Eric Pelham:** p. 16; **Cressida Pemberton Piggot:** p. 85; **Jonathan Plant:** p. 80; **Kevin J. Richardson:** pp. 2, 46, 60/1, 76, 81; **Ian Shaw:** p. 68; **Richard Surman:** p. 19; **Martin Trelawny:** p. 77; **Mike Warren:** pp. 26, 52; **Jeremy Whitaker:** p. 90; **Mike Williams:** pp. 9, 14, 21, 51, 66, front cover.

The publishers also wish to thank **Tony Lord** for his kind permission to reproduce the photographs on pages 23, 36, 54, 57, 74, 83, 87, back cover.

NOTES

N O T E S